Births, Marriages and Deaths on the Web

PART 1
General, Southern England, The Marches and Wales

Stuart A. Raymond

Published by
The Federation of Family History Societies (Publications) Ltd
Units 15-16, Chesham Industrial Centre
Oram Street, Bury,
Lancashire BL9 6EN

in association with
S.A. & M.J. Raymond
P.O.Box 35
Exeter, EX1 3YZ
Email: stuart@samjraymond.softnet.co.uk
Webpage: www.soft.net.uk/samjraymond/igb.htm

Copyright © Stuart A. Raymond

ISBNs:
Federation of Family History Socieies 1-86006 168 0
S.A. & M.J. Raymond: 1-899668-29-2

First Published 2002

Printed and bound by Alpha Print, Crawley Mill, Witney, Oxfordshire OX8 5TJ

Contents

Introduction	4	Sussex	61
General	5	Wiltshire	62
Berkshire	7	Worcestershire	65
Buckinghamshire	8	Wales	66
Channel Islands	9	Anglesey	67
Cornwall	10	Breconshire	67
Devon	15	Caernarvonshire	68
Dorset	19	Cardiganshire	68
Gloucestershire and Bristol	29	Carmarthenshire	69
Hampshire	34	Flint and Denbighshire	70
Herefordshire	37	Glamorganshire	71
Kent	39	Merionethshire	72
London & Middlesex	41	Monmouthshire	72
Oxfordshire	42	Montgomeryshire	73
Shropshire	43	Pembrokeshire	73
Somerset	44	Radnorshire	74
Surrey	60		

Introduction

The records of births, marriages and deaths are vital resources for family historians. A rapidly increasing number of transcripts and indexes of these records are now available on the internet, and it is the purpose of this directory to identify the many web-pages, and to indicate where they, and various introductory information, can be found. Pages rather than sites are listed, as one site can include pages for numerous different places - Genuki being the obvious example.

This directory is primarily concerned with civil registration and parish registers, although associated records such as bishops transcripts, marriage licences, *etc.* are also mentioned. I have not, except in a few cases, listed the pages of particular registry offices, nor have I included pages devoted solely to particular surnames. Monumental inscriptions and war memorials are the subjects of separate directories.

Arrangement of this directory is by county. Each county is sub-divided into sections on civil registration, introductory pages on parish and non-parochial registers, county-wide indexes, collections of transcripts/indexes from a variety of places, pages relating to particular parishes, and a few other topics.

The titles of each web-page are given as they appear on the page; if no title is given on the page I have indicated this by enclosing my own wording in square brackets. If the title does not indicate the period covered I have tried to indicate this in a note. If the page is an index, rather than a transcript, this is also noted (although not entirely consistently). Where the web-page is taken from a book, a brief bibliographic note is included.

It is noticeable that, although a few facsimiles of published registers have been mounted on the web, there are virtually no facsimiles of the original documents. It is therefore, necessary to repeat the exhortation with which all good genealogical authors encourage their readers: check your sources! A transcript or index is only as accurate as the transcriber or indexer. Some are very good indeed; others are awful! If at all possible, you should always go back to the original record and check it.

This directory is equally liable to human error. If you are unable to find a URL listed here, you should enter either a part of the URL itself, or words from the title, into a search engine such as www.google.com. URL's change frequently, and no doubt a small proportion of those listed here will be out of date within a few months of publication. If you come across errors in this book, URL's that have changed, or new pages that ought to be listed, please let me know. It is hoped to produce new editions at frequent intervals, in order to help you keep track of the information currently available on the web.

This book has been typed by Cynthia Hanson, and seen through the press by Bob Boyd. My thanks go to them, and also to the officers of the Federation of Family History Society, whose support is vital to my work. My wife Marjorie, is also to be thanked for insisting that I should turn the computer off occasionally!

Stuart A. Raymond

General

- England and Wales: Birth Marriage and Death Records
  www.pro.gov.uk/research/easysearch/certificate_enquiriesEngland.htm
  Gateway to various Public Record Office leaflets

Civil Registration
- A Comedy of Errors Continued ... The Marriage Records of England and Wales
  globalgazette.net/gazfd/gazfd.38.htm
- Barbara's Registration Web Page: Certificate Information
  home.clara.net/dixons/Certificate/indexbd.htm
  General information on obtaining certificates
- Family History: General Register Office Indexes
  www.westsussex.gov.uk/RO/FamHis/FHGRO%20Indexes.htm
  Indexes for the whole country available at the West Sussex Record Office
- Free BMD
  freebmd.rootsweb.com
  Project to index civil registration records, currently focused on the period 1837-1900
- General Register Office Indexes
  www.hants.gov.uk/record-office/gro.html
  Prepared by the Hampshire Record Office, but of country-wide interest.
- General Register Offices Indexes
  www.shropshire-cc.gov.uk/research.nsf
  Click on 'What we hold' and 'General Register Office Index'
  Explains some reasons for failing to find entries. Prepared by Shropshire Records, but of General Interest
- A Guide to Civil Registration in Great Britain
  www.gmcro.co.uk/family_history/st_caths.htm
  On the site of Greater Manchester County Record Office
- On-line Historical Gazetteer
  www.geog.gmw.ac.uk/gbhgis/gaz/rd_chan.html
  Registration District boundary changes 1850-1919
- Civil Registration: Vital Change: Birth Marriage and Death Registration in the 21st Century
  www.official-documents.co.uk/document.cm53/5355/5355.pdf
  Government proposals for the future of the service
- Government White Paper: Civil Registration: Vital Changes
  www.ffhs.org.uk/Societies/Liaison/WhitePaper.htm
  The F.F.H.S. response to the White Paper
- General Registration Office: Registration Review 2002: Planning the Society of Genealogists Response
  www.sog.org.uk/files/cm5355plan.html
- England and Wales Civil Registration Index 1837-1900
  www.ancestry.co.uk/search/rectype/vital/freebmd/main.htm
  Offers searches of the *FreeBMD* database (see above)
- Ordering Birth Registration Certificates from England and Wales using the LDS Family History Centre's Resources
  www.oz.net/~markhow/ukbirths.htm
- The St. Catherine's Marriage Index
  www.cs.ncl.ac.uk/genuki/StCathsTranscriptions
  Introduction to a collection of transcriptions, some of which are listed individually under appropriate counties in this directory

Parish & Non-Parochial Registers: Introductory Pages
- English Parish Registers
  freepages.genealogy.rootsweb.com/~engregisters
  General introduction, with advice on the process of transcription
- Parish Registers
  www.jaydax.co.uk/genlinks/registers.html
  General discussion, especially of northern registers
- Parish Registers (and nonconformist records), England and Wales
  www.familyrecords.gov.uk/parishenglandwales.htm
- Transcribing Parish Registers
  freepages.genealogy.rootsweb.com/~engregisters/registers/index.html
- Catholic Central Library Mission Registers
  www.catholic-library.org.uk/registers.html
  List of Roman Catholic register transcripts available

- The Library, Friend's House, London: Genealogical Sources
  www.quaker.org.uk/library/geneal.htm
  Includes information on the important Quaker 'digests' of births, marriages and deaths.
- Births, Marriages and Deaths at Sea
  www.pro.gov.uk/leaflets/Riindex.asp
  Click on title
- Births, Marriages and Deaths Overseas
  ihr.sas.ac.uk/gh/overseas.htm
  Leaflet from Guildhall Library, London

Indexes
- IGI Batch Numbers
  freepages.genealogy.rootsweb.com/~tyeroots/index4.html
  Introduction to an important database, with lists of batch numbers
- IGI Batch Numbers: British Isles and North America
  freepages.genealogy.rootsweb.com/~hughwallis/IGIBatchNumbers.htm
- The LDS Family Search © Website: Using the Batch Numbers
  globalgazette.net/gazfd/gazfd36.htm
- Batches Extracted from Dr. William's Non-Conformist Registers
  freepages.genealogy.rootsweb.com/~hughwallis/IGISpecialBatches.htm#DrWilliams
- Boyds Marriage Index 1538-1840
  www.englishorigins.com/bmi-details.html
- Cemetery Records: United Kingdom & Ireland Records
  userdb.rootsweb.com/uki
  Database with thousands of burial records
- FreeREG
  freereg.rootsweb.com/index.htm
  Project to provide free internet searches of parish registers
- The Institute of Heraldic and Genealogical Studies: Library Search Facilities
  www.ihgs.ac.uk/library/search__facilities.php
  Lists a variety of indexes to registers, *etc.* held by the Institute

- National Burial Index for England and Wales
  www.ffhs.org.uk/General/Projects/NBI.htm
  Details of a major project to index burials on CD
- Pedigree and People of the UK
  web.ukonline.co.uk/sheila.jones/ppp.htm
  Lists over 400 indexes, including many compiled from parish registers and inscriptions. The indexes themselves can be searched off-line
- Parish and Probate Records
  www.allvitalrecords.com/ukisearch.asp
  Database of 15,000,000+ records from England, Wales, Scotland and Ireland
- Ted Wildy's Marriage Witness Index
  www.genuki.org.uk/mwi/
- Marriage Witness Indexes
  members.optushome.com.au/guthrigg/mwi.htm
- Marriage Witness Indexes F.A.Q.
  homepages.ihug.co.nz/~hughw/mwifaq.html
- UK & Ireland Genealogy Collection
  www.allvitalrecords.com/ukisearch.asp
  Searchable database of over 15,000,000 names from (mainly) published parish registers and probate indexes

Marriage Licences
- Marriage Licence Allegations Index 1694-1850: Vicar-General and Faculty Office
  www.englishorigins.com/mla-details.html

Transcripts on the Web
- Parish Registers
  freepages.genealogy.rootsweb.com/~pinks
  Collection of transcripts from various counties
- UK Transcriptions Web-Site
  uk-transcriptions.accessgenealogy.com
  Collection of parish register transcripts, *etc.,* separately listed below

- United Kingdom Genealogy: Parish Registers
  www.uk-genealogy.org.uk/Registers/index.html
  Collection of parish registers available on the web, and listed separately elsewhere in this directory. Some also available on CD

Publications
- English Parish Records
  shops.ancestry.com/subcat.asp?shopid=126&CatID=520
  Parish registers on CD from Ancestry.com
- Review of Ancestry.com's English Parish Record CD's
  www.ancestry.com/library/view/columns/extra/4751.asp
- Archive CD Books: Church & Cemetery Registers
  www.rod-neep.co.uk/books/types/registers/
  General discussion of registers and transcripts which are being published on CD
- England and Wales Genealogy & History CD ROMS
  globalgenealogy.com/countries/england/cdrom.html
  Includes many registers on CD
- British Isles CD-Roms
  www.quintinpublications.com/cdengland.html
  Includes many parish registers on CD
- National Index of Parish Registers
  www.soft.net.uk/samjraymond/natipareg.html
  Details of the authoritative published guide to the whereabouts of original registers and transcripts
- TWR Computing
  www.twr computing.freeserve.co.uk
  Many parish registers on CD for sale

Miscellaneous
- Latin Words
  www.genealogy.doun.org/transcriptions/help/latin_words.php
  Commonly found in parish registers
- Prohibited Marriages
  www.badsey.net/history/prohib.htm
  List from the *Book of Common Prayer,* 1662

Berkshire

Civil Registration
- Registration Districts in Berkshire
  www.fhsc.org.uk/genuki/reg/brk.htm
  Between 1837 and 1930
- Wokingham Registration Service
  www.wokingham.gov.uk/registrars

Parish & Non-Parochial Registers, Introductory Pages & Lists
- Berkshire Parish Registers
  www.berksfhs.org.uk/projects/BerkshireParishRegisterProject.htm
  Transcription project, listing a few published registers
- Berkshire
  www.sog.org.uk/prc/berkshire.html
  Parish registers, printed, typescript, *etc.,* in the library of the Society of Genealogists
- Quaker Family History Society: Berkshire
  www.rootsweb.com/~engqfhs/Research/counties/berks.htm
  Notes on Quaker records

Indexes
- Berkshire, England: Parish and Probate Records
  www.ancestry.lycos.com/search/rectype/inddbs/5844.htm
  Database compiled from published registers *etc.*
- Berkshire Burial Index
  www.berksfhs.org.uk/berkshire/BerkshireBurialIndex.htm
  Lists parishes covered
- IGI Batch Numbers: Berkshire Batch Numbers
  freepages.genealogy.rootsweb.com/~tyeroots/berkshire.html
- IGI Batch Numbers for Berkshire, England
  freepages.genealogy.rootsweb.com/~hughwallis/IGIBatchNumbers/CountyBerkshire.htm

Appleford
- Transcript of Bishops' transcripts for Appleford, Berkshire, 1563-1835/7
  www.btinternet.com/~PBenyon/Den/Aplford/Index.html
  freepages.genealogy.rootsweb.com/~pbtyc/Den/Aplford/Index.html

Cockfield
- An index of Names of Burials at Cockfield 1578-1799
  cockfield.freeservers.com/contact.html
  Names only

Cookham
- Transcript of Bishops' transcripts for Cookham, Berkshire 1607-1635: Holy Trinity
  freepages.genealogy.rootsweb.com/~pbtyc/Den/Cookham/Index.html

- Index to Transcript of Bishops' transcripts for Cookham, Berkshire.
  www.btinternet.com/~PBenyon/Den/Cookham/Index.html
  Transcripts and indexes, 1607-35

Lambourne
- Index to the Transcript of Baptisms for the Parish Register for Lambourne, Berkshire
  freepages.genealogy.rootsweb.com/~pbtyc/Den/Lambrn/Index.html
  1560-1837

Buckinghamshire

Civil Registration
- Registration Districts in Buckinghamshire
  www.fhsc.org.uk/genuki/reg/bkm.htm
  Between 1837 and 1930

Parish and Non-Parochial Registers: Introductory Pages & Lists
- Centre for Buckinghamshire Studies. Parish Registers Index
  www.buckscc.gov.uk/archives/parishes/index.stm
  List of registers held

- Parish Records Listing
  met.open.ac.uk/group/kaq/bgs.htm
  List of transcripts held by Buckinghamshire Genealogical Society; also shows Buckinghamshire coverage in the I.G.I.

- Buckinghamshire
  www.sog.org.uk/prc/buckingham.html
  Parish registers, printed, typescript, *etc.,* in the library of the Society of Genealogists

- Quaker Family History Society: Buckinghamshire
  www.rootsweb.com/~engqfhs/Research/counties/bucks.htm
  Notes on Quaker records

Indexes
- Baptisms Database
  www.bucksfhs.org.uk/dbap0001.htm
  Offline searches available from Buckinghamshire Family History Society

- Marriages Database
  www.bucksfhs.org.uk/dmar0001.htm
  Offline searches available from Buckinghamshire Family History Society. Covers all available parish register entries 1538-1837

- Burials Database
  www.bucksfhs.org.uk/dbur0001.htm
  Offline searches available from Buckinghamshire Family History Society

- Buckinghamshire, England, Parish and Probate Records
  www.ancestry.com/search/locality/dbpage.htm?t=3257&c=3251&co=0&y=0&dbid=5847
  Database from published registers

- IGI Batch Numbers: Buckinghamshire Batch Numbers
  freepages.genealogy.rootsweb.com/~tyeroots/bucking.html

- IGI Batch Numbers for Buckingham, England
  freepages.genealogy.rootsweb.com/~hughwallis/IGIBatchNumbers/CountyBuckingham.htm

Maids Moreton
- The Parish of Maids Moreton
  www.parishregisters.co.uk/
  Click on 'Buckinghamshire' and 'Maids Moreton'. Includes baptisms 1817-1878, marriages 1760-1857, and burials 1809-1867; also various other entries for the families of Bailey, Hands, Knibbs and Tyrrell

Mentmore
- The Parish of Mentmore
  www.parishregisters.co.uk/
  Click on 'Buckinghamshire' and 'Mentmore'. Includes selected baptisms, marriages and burials, 1643-1893

Moulsoe
- The Parish of Moulsoe
  www.parishregisters.co.uk/
  Click on 'Buckinghamshire' and 'Moulsoe'. Includes baptisms 1667-1686, marriages 1690-1706, & burials 1667-1720.

Westbury
- The Parish of Bishop's Westbury
  www.parishregisters.co.uk
  Click on 'Buckinghamshire' and 'Westbury'. Covers 1558-1780

Channel Islands

Parish & Non-Parochial Registers: Introductory Pages & Lists

- Parish Registers of the Channel Islands
  user.itl.net/~glen/ClResearch.html#faq2
  List

- Channel Islands
  www.sog.org.uk/prc/channelislands.htm
  Parish register, printed, typescript, *etc.,* in the library of the Society of Genealogists

- Quaker Family History Society: Channel Islands
  www.rootsweb.com/~engqfhs/Research/counties/channel.htm

Cornwall

Civil Registration
- Family History in Cornwall: Cornwall Registration Service can Help You
  www.cornwall.gov.uk/ab-hi31.htm
  Includes list of registration districts and parishes

- Registration Districts in Cornwall
  www.fhsc.org.uk/genuki/reg/cnw.htm
  Between 1837 and 1930.

- [St. Catherine's House Marriage Index, Jan-March, 1849. District 9. Cornwall/Devon]
  www.cs.ncl.ac.uk/genuki/StCathsTranscriptions/CATH4909.TXT

Parish and Non-Parochial Registers: Introductory Pages and Lists
See also Devon

- Cornish Parish Registers: church (parish) registers & Bishops transcripts
  www.cornwallfhs.com/churchrecs.htm
  Introduction from Cornwall Family History Society

- Finding out about Family History: Parish Registers & other Registers
  www.cornwall.gov.uk/history/famhist/ab-le03c.htm
  In Cornwall Record Office

- Cornwall Library Service: a list of transcripts available
  www.cornwall.gov.uk/library/de-02zl.htm
  Mainly a list of published registers

- Primary Sources: Cornwall's Parish Registers
  lightning.prohosting.com/~cornwall/registers.html
  Introductory page, with list of unfilmed parishes

- Cornwall
  www.sog.org.uk/prc/cm.html
  Parish registers, printed, typescript, *etc.*, in the library of the Society of Genealogists

- Quaker Family History Society: Cornwall
  www.rootsweb.com/~engqfhs/Research/counties/cornwall.htm
  Notes on Quaker records

Indexes
- Cornish 19th century marriages
  www.geocities.com/ausich2000/
  Index in progress

- Cornwall, England: Parish & Probate Records
  www.ancestry.lycos.com/search/rectype/inddbs/5860.htm
  Database including extracts from numerous parish registers

- IGI Batch Numbers: Cornwall Batch Numbers
  freepages.genealogy.rootsweb.com/~tyeroots/cornwall.html

- IGI Batch Numbers for Cornwall, England
  freepages.genealogy.rootsweb.com/~hughwallis/IGIBatchNumbers/CountyCornwall.htm

Transcript Collection on the Web
- Online Parish Clerks - Cornwall
  www.parsons1998.freeserve.co.uk/opc.htm
  Project to co-ordinate transcription of Cornish parish registers, with list of parishes, email addresses of parish coordinators, and links to relevant web-sites.

Publications
- Parish Transcriptions
  www.cornish-forefathers.com/fiche.htm
  Parish registers available on CD from the Cornish Forefathers Society

Strays
- Born Cornwall, Died ...
  chrisuphill.tripod.com/bcd.htm
  Records of people born in Cornwall but died elsewhere

Look-ups
- Cornwall Look-up Exchange
  www.tridwr.demon.co.uk/lookup/
  Many offers to look-up information from Cornish parish registers

Budock
- Marriages at Budock: from Phillimore Parish Registers
  www.uk-genealogy.org.uk/england/Cornwall/towns/b/Budock/index.html
  Facsimile of published transcript. Covers 1653-1812

Caerhays
- Caerhays Marriages from 1837-1915
  www.gorran-haven.com/caerhays.htm

Carbis Bay
See West Penwith

Egloskerry
- Sample PDF File: Egloskerry, Cornwall 1574-1812
  homepages.rootsweb.com/~rodneep/books/samples/0122samp.pdf

Gorran
- Gorran Church Baptisms
  www.gorran-haven.com/baptisms.htm
  For an alphabetical index, see /gorbapt.htm
  Covers 1662-1998

- Gorran Parish Baptisms Alphabetically
  www.gorran-haven.com/gorbapt.htm
  18-19th c.

- Gorran Parish Church Marriages: alphabetically
  www.gorran-haven.com/gormar.htm
  18-19th c.

- Gorran Church Marriages
  www.gorran-haven.com/marriage.htm
  Covers 1931-99

- St. Gorran Parish Burials alphabetically
  www.gorran-haven.com/gorbur.htm
  18-19th c.

- St. Gorran Church Burials
  www.gorran-haven.com/burials.htm
  Burials 1912-89

- Gorran Burial Records 1950-2002
  www.gorran-haven.com/gobur.htm

- Gorran Haven Chapel Baptisms
  www.gorran-haven.com/gorchapel.htm
  19th century

Gulval
- Gulval Marriages 1883-1902
  www.parsons1998.freeserve.co.uk/gulvalm.htm
  See also West Penwith

Gwinear
- Gwinear, Cornwall: OPC Project
  www.westcountrygenealogy.com/cornwall/gwinear/
  Burials 1702-49 at present available online; more to follow. List of registers, transcripts, and locations; lookups offered.

Gwithean
- The Gwithean Page
  www.lanset.com/azazella/gwithian__page.html
  Baptisms 1560-1769; marriages 1560-1759; burials 1560-1757

Halsetown
See West Penwith

Illogan
- Parish Records
  www.saint-illogan.org.uk/records.htm
  From the sexton's records of burial plots, from 1895

Kenwyn
- Kenwyn Parish Registers: some Baptisms
  www.genuki.org.uk/big/eng/Cornwall/Kenwyn/Baptisms.html
  Early 19th c.

- Kenwyn Parish Registers: some marriages
  www.genuki.org.uk/big/eng/Cornwall/Kenwyn/Marriages.html
  18-19th c.

- Kenwyn Parish Registers: some Banns 1772-1784
  www.genuki.org.uk/big/eng/Cornwall/Kenwyn/Banns.html

- Kenwyn Parish Registrs: some burials
  www.genuki.org.uk/big/eng/Cornwall/Kenwyn/Burials.htm

Lamorran
- Lamorran Parish Register Index
  www.cornish-ancestors.co.uk/Lamorran/Parish%20Registers/index_parish_registers.htm
  Not yet compiled, but in prospect

Lelant
- (Uny) Lelant, Cornwall On-line Parish Clerk
  chrisuphill.tripod.com/lelant.htm
  Indexes to births, marriages and deaths, 17-19th c.
  See also West Penwith

Lewannick
- Marriages at Lewannick, from Phillimore Parish Registers
  www.uk-genealogy.org.uk/england/Cornwall/towns/l/Lewannick/index.html
  Covers 1675-1812

Ludgvan
See West Penwith

Madron
- Sample Page of Marriages from the Madron Parish Registers
  www.cornwall-net.co.uk/cornishroots/35.htm
  From the Phillimore transcription, 1626-35
  See also West Penwith

Mevagissey
- Mevagissey Baptisms alphabetically
  www.gorran-haven.com/mevbapt.htm
  18-19th c.

- Mevagissey Chapel Baptisms
  www.gorran-haven.com/mevachapel.htm
  18-19th c.

- Mevagissey Marriages from 1837-1906
  www.gorran-haven.com/mevamar.htm

- Mevagissey Burials
  www.gorran-haven.com/mevbur.htm
  Continued on 2 further pages. Covers 1882-1952

Morvah
See West Penwith

Newlyn
See West Penwith

Paul
See West Penwith

Pendeen
See West Penwith

Penzance
See West Penwith

Phillack
- Phillack Parish
  freepages.genealogy.rootsweb.com/~jwheeler/parishrecords.htm
  Includes baptisms, 1560-1819, marriages 1813-1839, and burials 1560-1829.

Philleigh
- Philleigh: Parish Records
  www.cornish-ancestors.co.uk/Philleigh/Parish%20Registers/index_parish_registers.htm
  Indexes

Roche
- Roche Cornwall Resource Site: Bap.Mar.Bur.
  www.hmpage.net/west/page1.php
  Parish register lookups available

St. Austell
- St. Austell Wedding Entries
  homepages.rootsweb.com/~marcie/kernow/marriage.html
  Covers 1564-71

St. Blazey
- St. Blazey Parish O.P.C.
  freepages.genealogy.rootsweb.com/~kayhin/blaz.html
  Births/baptisms, marriages and deaths/burials from various sources.

St. Buryan
See West Penwith

St. Colan
- Marriages at St. Colan, from Phillimore Parish Registers
  www.uk-genealogy.org.uk/england/Cornwall/towns/s/StColan/index.html
  Covers 1665-1812

St. Columb Minor
- Marriages at St. Columb Minor, from Phillimore Parish Registers
  www.uk-genealogy.org.uk/england/Cornwall/towns/s/StColumbMinor/index.html
  Facsimile. Covers 1560-1812

St. Erth
- Dee's St. Erth, Cornwall, UK Genealogy Page
  freepages.genealogy.rootsweb.com/~sterth
  Includes baptisms, 1563-1900, marriages 1563-1960, and burials 1565-1960

St. Ewe
- St. Ewe Chapel Baptisms
  www.gorran-haven.com/stewechapel.htm

- St. Ewe Baptisms Alphabetically
  www.gorran-haven.com/stewe.htm

St. Gennys
- St. Gennys OPC
  freepages.genealogy.rootsweb.com/~winnacott/opc.htm
  Lookups of baptisms and burials offered

St. Gluvias
- Marriages at St. Gluvias from Phillimore Parish Registers
  www.uk-genealogy.org.uk/england/Cornwall/towns/s/StGluvias/index.html
  Facsimile of published register. Covers 1599 to 1812

St. Issey
- Marriages at St. Issey, from Phillimore Parish Registers
  www.uk-genealogy.org.uk/england/Cornwall/towns/s/StIssey/index.html
  Facsimile of published register. Covers 1596-1812

St. Ive
- St. Ive Parish
  www.geocities.com/st_ivecornwall/
  Brief list of registers; includes baptisms 1800-1808 and burials 1800-1820. In progress

St. Ives
- Marriages at St. Ives, from Phillimore Parish Registers
  www.uk-genealogy.org.uk/england/Cornwall/towns/s/StIves/index.html
  Facsimile of published register. Covers 1653-1812

- Parish Burial Register for St. Ives, Cornwall, 1653 to 1753
  lightning.prohosting.com/~cornwall/data/stivbalu.txt

See also West Penwith

St. Keverne
- Burials in St. Keverne, Cornwall
  freepages.genealogy.rootsweb.com/%7Eframland/stk/stkind.htm
  Indexes for 1597-1836 and 1837-1855

St. Levan
See West Penwith

St. Martin in Meneage
- St. Martin in Meneage Online Parish Clerk
  www.westcountrygenealogy.com/cornwall/st_martin/
  Includes marriages 1571-1812 online; lookups available for burials, later marriages, and monumental inscriptions.

St. Mawgan
- Parish Registers: St. Mawgan church
  www.westcountrygenealogy.com/cornwall/mawgan/parishrecords.htm
  List of registers available on film at L.D.S. Family History Centres. Lookups available.

- Marriages at St. Mawgan in Meneage, from Phillimore Parish Registers
  www.uk-genealogy.org.uk/england/Cornwall/towns/s/StMawgan/index.html
  Facsimile of published register. Covers 1563-1812

St. Stephen in Brannel
- St. Stephen in Brannel Parish Register Page
  www.sartorelli.gen.nz/parishregister/ststepheninbrannel.html
  Baptisms 1690-1819; marriages 1740-1859; burials 1690-1749. Searchable database.

- St. Stephen in Brannel, Cornwall, England
  community-2.webtv.net/geniefriend/StStepheninBrannel/
  Burials 1695-1822; marriages 1608-1843. In progress.

Sancreed
See West Penwith

Sennen
- Sennen Parish Registers
  sennencornwall.tripod.com/sennen__registers.htm
  Baptisms 1700-73; marriages 1699-1837; burials 1699-1812.
See also West Penwith

South Hill
- South Hill Parish Family History Site
  www.geocities.com/southhillcornwall/
  Baptisms 1614-1900; marriages 1566-1900; burials 1614-1900.

Tintagel
- Tintagel Parish, Cornwall, UK
  members.aol.com/Dprsns827/Tintagel/OPC.htm
  Parish register lookups offered

Towednack
See West Penwith

Trevenson
- Trevenson Church Burial Register
  www.saint-illogan.org.uk/burials__trevn.html
  Covers from 1880

Treverbyn
- Treverbyn Burials (selected extractions)
  homepages.rootsweb.com/~marcie/kernow/trevburials.html
  Covers 1798-1835

Uny Lelant
See Lelant

Veryan
- Veryan Mailing List Home Pages
  www.cornish-ancestors.co.uk/Veryan
  Click on 'Parish Records' for an index in progress.

West Penwith
- West Penwith Resources: Baptisms
  www.parsons1998.freeserve.co.uk/wpenbapt.htm
  List of original registers, transcripts, *etc.,* for St. Buryan, Gulval, St. Ives, Halsetown, St. Just in Penwith, Pendeen, Lelant, Carbis Bay, St. Levan, Ludgvan, Madron, Penzance, Morvah, Paul, Newlyn, Sancreed, Sennen, Towednack, and Zennor.

- Kernow's West Penwith Genealogy: Parish Registers
  freepages.genealogy.rootsweb.com/~kernow/parish.htm
  Extracts for selected names from the registers of Uny Lelant, Phillack Towednack, Zennor and Gulval

- West Penwith Resources: marriages
  www.parsons1998.freeserve.co.uk/wpenmar.htm

- West Penwith Resources: Burials
  www.parsons1998.freeserve.co.uk/wpenbur.htm

Zennor
See West Penwith

Devon

Civil Registration
- Registration Districts in Devonshire
  www.fhsc.org.uk/genuki/reg/dev.htm
  Between 1837 and 1930

Parish & Non-Parochial Registers: Introductory Pages and Lists
- Devon Parish, Non-parochial and civil registers in the Devon Record Office, Exeter, North Devon Record Office, and City of Plymouth and West Devon Record Office
  www.devon.gov.uk/dro/register/homepage.html
- Copying of Parish Registers: an information note provided by the Devon Record Office
  www.cs.ncl.ac.uk/genuki/DEV/ParishRegisters.html
- Parish registers in the Devon Record Office
  www.cs.ncl.ac.uk/genuki/DEV/DevonCRO/PR-Holdings.htm
- Parish Registers in the Devon & Cornwall Record Society's Collection
  www.cs.ncl.ac.uk/genuki/DEV/DCRS-Holdings.html
  Collection of transcripts for both counties held in the Society's library
- The Devon and Cornwall Record Society: a shelflist of the collection
  www.devon.gov.uk/library/locstudy/dcrs.html
  Mainly parish register transcripts
- Devonshire
  www.sog.org.uk/prc/dev.html
  Parish registers, printed, typescript, *etc.*, in the library of Society of Genealogists
- Quaker Family History Society: Devon
  www.rootsweb.com/~engqfhs/Research/counties/devon.htm
  Notes on Quaker records
- English Parish Records Collection 1531-1906
  www.mun.ca/mha/genealog.html#English
  Brief note on a collection of fiche records from S.W.England, especially Devon, Dorset, Somerset and Hampshire, at the Maritime History Archive, University of Newfoundland

Indexes
- Parishes covered by Boyd's Marriage Index: Devon
  www.englishorigins.com/bmi-parishstats.asp?county=Devon
- IGI Batch Numbers: Devon Batch Numbers
  freepages.genealogy.rootsweb.com/~tyeroots/devon.html
- IGI Batch Numbers for Devon, England
  freepages.genealogy.rootsweb.com/~hughwallis/IGIBatchNumbers/CountyDevon__(A-M).htm
  Continued at **/CountyDevon__(N-Z).htm**
- IGI Batch Numbers for Devon
  www.freenetpages.co.uk/hp/mjcurtis/igi.htm
- IGI Batch Numbers for Devon Parish Baptisms
  www.owlscottage.co.uk/morrish/DEVbapbatch.htm

Publications
- Devon Family History Society Publications
  www.devonfhs.org.uk
  Click on 'Publications'. Many records of births, marriages and deaths have been published by the society and are listed here, as are various indexes available for searching
- Dartmoor Press
  www.dartmoorpress.clara.net
  Many transcripts of parish registers for the Dartmoor area on CD

Transcript Collections on the Web
- Devon Online Parish Clerks and One-Place Studies
  www.cs.ncl.ac.uk/genuki/DEV/OPCproject.html

Abbots Bickington
- St. James Church, Abbots Bickington
  www.sutcomberecords.co.uk
  Click on 'contents' and title

Aveton Gifford
- Aveton Gifford Parish Register
  www-civ.eng.cam.ac.uk/agrecord.htm
  Note on a transcription project, with list of surnames and their frequency

Branscombe
- The Parish Registers and Churchwardens Accounts
  www.geocities.com/micogenealogy/johnmico.html
  Discussion of the Branscombe register

- A Guide to the church of St. Winifred, Branscombe: the Parish Registers and Churchwardens accounts
  www.geocities.com/Athens/2155/register.html
  Discussion rather than a transcript

Brixham
- Brixham St. Mary Burials 1813-1837
  users.hunterlink.net.au/~ddhms/Lookup/brixham__html
  Surname list

- Brixham Heritage Museum
  www.brixhamheritage.org.uk
  Click on 'Brixham People' for lists of surnames from selected churchyard inscriptions and non-conformist burial registers

Buckfastleigh
- Buckfastleigh OPC: Wesleyan Methodist Baptism Registers 1857-1900: Surname Index
  www.express.demon.co.uk/opc/baps__idx.html
  Full transcript coming soon

Churchstanton
- Churchstanton Baptisms 1662-1902
  www.genuki.org.uk/big/eng/SOM/Churchstanton/BapChu.html
  Index

- Churchstanton Marriage Banns 1766-1791
  www.genuki.org.uk/big/eng/SOM/Churchstanton/BanChu.html

- Churchstanton Marriages 1662-1901
  www.genuki.org.uk/big/eng/SOM/Churchstanton/MarChu.html
  Index

- Churchstanton, St. Peter & St. Paul Burials 1662-1902
  www.genuki.org.uk/big/eng/SOM/Churchstanton/BurChu.html

- Churchstanton, St. Peter & St. Paul, Somerset (formerly Devon): Burials 1678-1902
  homepages.rootsweb.com/~mwi/Stpeter__txt

- Churchstanton, St. Peter & St. Paul, Burials 1662-1902
  www.genuki.org.uk/big/eng/SOM/Churchstanton/BurChu.html

Churston Ferrers
- Churston Ferrers burials 1800-1837
  users.hunterlink.net.au/~ddhms/Lookup/churston.html
  Surname list

Diptford
- Diptford, Devon: Baptisms (selected names)
  freepages.genealogy.rootsweb.com/~valhender/transcripts/diptford/diptford__1.html

  Covers 1738-1895

Ermington
- Ermington Parish Register Extracts
  freepages.genealogy.rootsweb.com/~lynnash/parishext.htm
  Under construction

Exeter
- Registers of Exeter Cathedral
  www.uk-genealogy.org.uk/england/Devon/Cathedral/index.html
  Facsimile of the volume published by Devon & Cornwall Record Society

Filleigh
- Filleigh Baptism 1813-37
  www.cs.ncl.ac.uk/genuki/DEV/Filleigh/Baptisms1813-37.html
  Continued for 1838-75 at **/Baptisms1838-75.html**

- Filleigh Burials 1813-37
  www.cs.ncl.ac.uk/DEV/Filleigh/Burials1813-37.html
  Continued for 1838-99 at **/Burials1838-99.html**

Harberton
- Parish Register Transcripts
  freepages.genealogy.rootsweb.com/~valhender/opc/harberton.htm#parish

  For Harberton; selected extracts only

- Harberton, Devon, Baptisms (selected names)
  freepages.genealogy.rootsweb.com/%7Evalhender/transcripts/harberton/harberton__1.html
- Harberton, Devon: Marriages (selected names)
  freepages.genealogy.rootsweb.com/~valhender/transcripts/harberton/harbertonmarriages__1.html
- Harberton, Devon, Burials (selected names)
  freepages.genealogy.rootsweb.com/~valhender/transcripts/harberton/harbertonburials__1.html

Hartland
- Hartland Births A-C
  members.rogers.com/trwatson/Hartland/Births%20A-C/births__a-c.htm
  Index to various sources 17-19th c. Continued on 2 further pages.
- Hartland Marriages
  members.rogers.com/trwatson/Hartland/Marriages/hartland__marriages.htm
  Index, 17-19th c., to miscellaneous sources
- Hartland Deaths
  members.rogers.com/trwatson/Hartland/Deaths/hartlanddeaths.htm
  Index to miscellaneous sources, 16-20th c.

High Bickington
- High Bickington Parish Burial Records
  www.high-bickington.org.uk/burialsindex.htm
  Covers 1813-79

Ide
- Ide Page
  homepage.ntlworld.com/sjfroud/Ide.html
  Baptisms 1735-1843; banns 1754-1823; marriages 1734-1837; burials 1736-1856; gravestone inscriptions, *etc.* In progress.

Kingsbridge
- Kingsbridge Burials 1631-1637; 1635-1797
  www.coleridge100.freeserve.co.uk/burials/bur__king/dataindex.htm

Luppitt
- Luppitt: Parish, Church and People
  homepages.ntlworld.com/greenink/luppitt/text/res/otherres.htm
  Baptisms 1766-1920, marriages 1724-1920; burials 1813-63, monumental inscriptions

Malborough
- Malborough Burials 1813-1837
  www.terrypar.dircon.co.uk/bur__mb/dataindex.htm

Marldon
- St. John the Baptist Church in Marldon, Devon
  www.geocities.com/Athens/Acropolis/3033/marldon.html
  List of surnames on gravestones

Newton Abbot
- Providence Independent Chapel Parish Register (births): Newton Abbot 1817-1837
  www.wotton.accessgenealogy.com/reg1.htm

Northam
- Northam Baptisms A-K (1748-1788)
  www.cs.ncl.ac.uk/genuki/DEV/Northam/NorthamBaptismsA-K.html
  For L-Y, see **/NorthamBaptismsL-Y.html**
- Northam Marriage Register Extracts
  www.cs.ncl.ac.uk/genuki/DEV/Northam/NorthamMarriages.html
  Extracts relating mainly to husbands from other places
- Northam Marriages 1748 to 1812: Index
  www.cs.ncl.ac.uk/genuki/DEV/Northam/NorthamMarriageIndex.html

Parracombe
- Register of Parracombe
  www.uk-genealogy.org.uk/england/Devon/towns/p/Parracombe/index.html
  Facsimile of a Devon and Cornwall Record Society publication

Peter Tavy
- Roger Meyrick's Peter Tavy Page: the Parish Registers
  dialspace.dial.pipex.com/town/terrace/xds53/parish.htm
  Notes on the webmaster's transcription project

Petrockstowe
- Petrockstowe One Place Genealogy: Parish registers: baptisms
  www.petrockstowe.co.uk/baptism.html
  Covers 1603-1810

- Petrockstowe One Place Genealogy: Parish Registers: marriages
  www.petrockstowe.co.uk/marriage.html
  Covers 1597-1766

- Petrockstowe One Place Genealogy: Parish Registers: burials
  www.petrockstowe.co.uk/burial.html
  Covers 1610-1807+

Plymouth
- Plymouth Marriage Middle Names
  members.rogers.com/stokedamerelopc/marriage__lookup__request.htm
- Holy Trinity, Plymouth, Devon. Baptisms (selected names)
  freepages.genealogy.rootsweb.com/~valhender/transcripts/holytrinity/holy%20trinity%20baptisms__1.html
- St. Peter, Plymouth, Devon; Baptisms (selected names)
  freepages.genealogy.rootsweb.com/~valhender/transcripts/peters/peterbap.html

Plymtree
- The Plymtree People Index 1611 to 1898 (and some earlier)
  users.hunterlink.net.au/~ddhms/Lookup/Plymtree.htm
  Surname index to a wide range of records, including the parish register.

- The Register of Plymtree, Devon
  www.uk-genealogy.org.uk/england/Devon/towns/p/Plymtree/index.html
  Facsimile of edition originally published by Devon & Cornwall Record Society

South Huish
- South Huish Burials 1813-1837
  www.terrypar.dircon.co.uk/bur__sh/data.htm

Stoke Damerel
- [Stoke Damerel registers held at Plymouth & West Devon Record Office].
  www.members.rogers.com/stokedamerelopc/DROinfo.htm
  Detailed list of parish registers on microfilm

- Stoke Damerel Baptisms: Selected names only.
  freepages.genealogy.rootsweb.com/~valhender/transcripts/stokedamerel/stokebaptisms__1.html

- Baptism Lookup Request
  members.rogers.com/stokedamerelopc/baptism__lookup__request.htm
  For Stoke Damerel, 1801-14

- Stoke Damerel Marriages: selected names only
  freepages.genealogy.rootsweb.com/~valhender/transcripts.stokedamerel/stokedamerelmar__1.html

Stoke Gabriel
- Stoke Gabriel, Devon, Baptisms (selected names)
  freepages.genealogy.rootsweb.com/~valhender/transcripts/stokegab/stokegabbapt.html

- Stoke Gabriel, Devon, burials (selected names)
  freepages.genealogy.rootsweb.com/~valhender/transcripts/stokegab/stokeburi.html

Sutcombe
- Sutcombe Village Records
  www.sutcomberecords.co.uk
  The parish register will shortly be added to this site

Upottery
- Some Selected Upottery Burials
  www.parkhouse.org.uk/upotteryburials.htm
  Selected surnames only, 17-19th c.

Dorset

Civil Registration
- Registration Districts in Dorset
  www.fhsc.org.uk/genuki/reg/dor.htm
  Between 1837 and 1930
- [St. Catherine's House Marriage Index, Jan-March, 1849. District 8. Dorset / Wiltshire]
  www.cs.ncl.ac.uk/genuki/StCathsTranscriptions/CATH4908.TXT

Parish & Non-Parochial Registers: Introductory Pages & Lists
See also Devon
- Dorset Archives Service: Dorset Parish Registers
  www.dorset-cc.gov.uk
  Go to 'A-Z Index', search 'Archives', click on 'Our Records' and 'Dorset Parish Register Guide online'. Includes list of registers held
- Dorset Parish Registers
  www.sdfhs.org/Library/dpr.htm
  List of transcripts *etc.,* held by Somerset & Dorset Family History Society
- Dorset
  www.sog.org.uk/prc/dor.html
  Parish registers, printed, typescript, *etc.,* in the library of the Society of Genealogists
- Quaker Family History Society: Dorset
  www.rootsweb.com/~engqfhs/Research/counties/dorset.htm
  Notes on Quaker records
- British Vital Records Index
  www.thedorsetpage.com/Genealogy/info/british__vri.htm
  Lists the Dorset parish registers indexed on the CD's

Indexes
- Services [of Dorset Family History Society]
  www.dorsetfhs.freeserve.co.uk/Services.htm
  Includes details of the society's parish register index
- IGI Batch Numbers for Dorset, England
  freepages.genealogy.rootsweb.com/~hughwallis/IGIBatchNumbers/CountyDorset.htm
- IGI Batch Numbers: Dorset Batch Numbers
  freepages.genealogy.rootsweb.com/~tyeroots/dorset.html

Transcript Collections on the Web
- The Blackmore Vale
  www.westcountrygenealogy.com/blackmore/
  Collection of parish register transcriptions
- Dorset Parish Transcriptions
  www.rootsweb.com/~engdorse/Dorset.html
  Pages containing contributed extracts (mainly brief) for many parishes, separately listed below
- Index of a few extracts from West Dorset Parish Registers, Wills, Admons., Phillimores, *etc.*
  www.btinternet.com/~PBenyon/W__Dorset/Index.html
  Collection of miscellaneous web pages, some of which are listed below

Look-Ups
- Dorset Parish Information Page
  www.melcombe.freeserve.co.uk/dorset/parish.htm
  Offers many look-ups of parish register information

Miscellaneous
- A Few Marriages extracted from various West Dorset and other Sources
  www.btinternet.com/~PBenyon/W__Dorset/W__Dorset__Mar.htm

Abbotsbury
- Dorset Parish Register Index: Parish of Abbotsbury: Abbotsbury Baptisms 1574-1812
  www.rootsweb.com/~engdorse/ABBOTSBURY.html
  Brief extracts only
- Dorset Parish Registers Index: Abbotsbury Marriages 1600-1800
  www.rootsweb.com/~engdorse/A/ABBOTSBURY1.html
  Brief extracts only

Affpuddle
- Dorset Parish Registers Index: Affpuddle, St. Laurence baptisms 1700-1900
  www.rootsweb.com/~engdorse/A/AFFPUDDLE.html
  Brief extracts only

Alderholt
- Dorset Parish Registers Index: Alderholt Parish; Alderholt Parish Marriages
  www.rootsweb.com/~engdorse/ALDERHOLT.html
  Brief extracts only

- Dorset Parish Register Index: Alderholt Parish Marriages 1800-1900
  www.rootsweb.com/~engdorse/A/ALDERHOLT1.html
  Brief extracts only

Allington
- Dorset Parish Registers Index: Allington Parish Baptisms 1700-1900
  www.rootsweb.com/~engdorse/A/ALLINGTON.html
  Brief extracts only

- A few Baptisms and Burials extracted from Allington, Dorset Parish Registers
  www.btinternet.com/~PBenyon/W__Dorset/Allington__Bap.htm
  18th c.

- Dorset Parish Registers Index: Allington Parish Burials 1700-1900
  www.rootsweb.com/~engdorse/ALLINGTON2.html
  Brief extracts only

Anderson
- Dorset Parish Registers Index: Anderson St. Michael Baptisms
  www.rootsweb.com/~engdorse/ANDERSON.html
  Brief extracts only

Arne
- Dorset Parish Registers Index: Arne Baptisms
  www.rootsweb.com/~engdorse/ARNE.html
  Brief extracts

Ashmore
- Dorset Parish Registers Index: Ashmore St. Nicholas Parish: Baptisms 1800-1900
  www.rootsweb.com/~engdorse/A/ASHMORE.html
  Brief extracts only

Askerswell
- Dorset Parish Registers Index: Askerswell Parish: Askerswell Baptisms 1700-1900
  www.rootsweb.com/~engdorse/ASKERSWELL.html
  Brief extracts only

Athelhampton
- Dorset Parish Registers Index: Athelhampton Parish Baptisms 1700-1900
  www.rootsweb.com/~engdorse/ATHELHAMPTON.html
  Brief extracts only

Batcombe
- Dorset Parish Registers Index: Batcombe Parish: Batcombe Parish Baptisms 1700-1900
  www.rootsweb.com/~engdorse/B/BATCOMBE.html
  Brief extracts only

Beaminster
- Dorset Parish Registers Index: Parish of Beaminster Baptisms 1585-1900
  www.rootsweb.com/~engdorse/B/BEAMINSTER.html
  Brief extracts only

Bere Regis
- Dorset Parish Registers Index: Bere Regis Parish
  www.rootsweb.com/~engdorse/BERE__REGIS.html
  Burials 1800-1895; brief extracts only

Bettiscombe
- Dorset Parish Registers Index: Bettiscombe Parish
  www.rootsweb.com/~engdorse/BETTISCOMBE.html
  Brief extracts only

Bincombe
- Dorset Parish Registers Index: Bincombe Parsih
  www.rootsweb.com/~engdorse/BINCOMBE.html
  Brief extracts only

Bishops Caundle
- Dorset Parish Registers Index: Bishops Caundle Parish
  www.rootsweb.com/~engdorse/BISHOPS_CAUNDLE.html
  Brief extracts only

Blandford Forum
- Dorset Parish Registers Index: Parish of Blandford Forum Marriages 1700-1900
  www.rootsweb.com/~engdorse/BLANDFORD_FORUM.html
  Brief extracts only

Blandford St. Mary
- Dorset Parish Registers: Blandford St. Mary Parish
  www.rootsweb.com/~engdorse/BLANDFORD_ST_MARY.html
  Brief extracts only

Bloxworth
- Dorset Parish Registers Index: Bloxworth Parish
  www.rootsweb.com/~engdorse/BLOXWORTH.html
  Brief extracts only

Bothenhampton
- Dorset Parish Registers Index: Bothenhampton Parish
  www.rootsweb.com/~engdorse/BOTHENHAMPTON.html
  Brief extracts only

Bradford Abbas
- Bradford Abbas Baptisms, Burials and Marriages 1572-1576 and 1579-1581
  www.melcombe.freeserve.co.uk/dorset/bradabbdm.htm
  From *Somerset and Dorset notes and queries* **17, 1923**
- **Dorset Parish Registers Index: Parish of Bradford Abbas**
  www.rootsweb.com/~engdorse/BRADFORD_ABBAS.html
  Brief extracts only

Bradford Peverell
- Bradford Peverell Baptisms Burials and Marriages 1572-1582
  www.melcombe.freeserve.co.uk/dorset/bradpevbdm.htm

- Dorset Parish Registers Index: Bradford Peverell Parish
  www.rootsweb.com/~engdorse/BRADFORD_PEVERELL.html
  Brief extracts only

Bradpole
- A few baptisms extracted from Bradpole, Dorset Parish Registers
  www.btinternet.com/~PBenyon/W_Dorset/Bradpole_Bap.htm
  18th c.
- Dorset Parish Registers Index: Bradpole Parish Baptisms 1700-1800
  www.rootsweb.com/~engdorse/BRADPOLE.html
  Brief extracts only

Branksome
- Baptisms, Burials and Marriages, St. Aldhelm's and All Saints, Branksome, 1895/7 transcribed by Helen Jones
  www.melcombe.freeserve.co.uk/brankbdm.htm

Bridport
- A Few Baptisms Extracted from Bridport, Dorset, Parish Registers
  www.btinternet.com/~PBenyon/W_Dorset/Bridport_Bap.htm
  18-19th c.
- A Few Burials extracted from Bridport, Dorset, Parish Registers
  www.btinternet.com/~PBenyon/W_Dorset/Bridport_Bur.htm
  18-19th c.
- Dates of Birth recorded in the Bridport Parish Registers for Dissenters in the Bridport Area, Dorset
  www.btinternet.com/~PBenyon/W_Dorset/Bridport_Diss.htm
- Dorset Parish Registers Index: St. Mary's, Bridport Parish Baptisms 1600-1900
  www.rootsweb.com/~engdorse/BRIDPORT.html
  Brief extracts only

Broadmayne
- Dorset Parish Registers Index: Broadmayne Parish
  www.rootsweb.com/~engdorse/BROADMAYNE.html
  Brief extracts only

Broadway
- Dorset Parish Registers Index: Broadway Parish
  www.rootsweb.com/~engdorse/BROADWAY.html
  Brief extracts only

Broadwinsor
- Some Broadwinsor Extracts from P.R's plus other bits that may be of interest
  www.btinternet.com/~PBenyon/W_Dorset/Broadwinsor_Snip.htm
  18-19th c.

- Dorset Parish Registers Index: Broadwinsor Parish
  www.rootsweb.com/~engdorse/BROADWINSOR.html
  Brief extracts only

Bryanston
- Dorset Parish Registers Index: Bryanston Parish
  www.rootsweb.com/~engdorse/BRYANSTON.html
  Brief extracts only

Buckland Newton
- Dorset Parish Registers Index: Buckland Newton Parish
  www.rootsweb.com/~engdorse/BUCKLAND_NEWTON%20.html
  Brief extracts only

Buckland Ripers
- Dorset Parish Registers Index: Buckland Ripers Parish
  www.rootsweb.com/~engdorse/BUCKLAND_RIPERS.html
  Brief extracts only

Burleston
- Dorset Parish Registers Index: Burleston Parish: Burleston Baptisms 1800-1900
  www.rootsweb.com/~engdorse/BURLESTON.html
  Brief extracts only

Burstock
- Dorset Parish Registers Index: Burstock Parish
  www.rootsweb.com/~engdorse/BURSTOCK.html
  Brief extracts only

- Some Marriages, Burials and Baptisms extracted from Burstock, Dorset, Parish Registers
  www.btinternet.com/~PBenyon/W_Dorset/Burstock_Bur.htm
  17-19th c.

Burton Bradstock
- Dorset Parish Registers Index: Burton Bradstock Parish
  www.rootsweb.com/~engdorse/BURTON_BRADSTOCK.html
  Brief extracts only

Canford Magna
- Dorset Parish Registers Index: Canford Magna Baptisms 1600-1900
  www.rootsweb.com/~engdorse/CANFORD_MAGNA.html
  Brief extracts only

Cann
- Dorset Parish Registers Index: Cann Parish
  www.rootsweb.com/~engdorse/CANN.html
  Brief extracts only

Castleton
- Dorset Parish Registers Index: Castleton Parish
  www.rootsweb.com/~engdorse/CASTLETON.html
  Brief extracts only

Cattistock
- Dorset Parish Registers Index: Cattistock Parish
  www.rootsweb.com/~engdorse/CATTISTOCK.html
  Brief extracts only

Caundle Marsh
- Dorset Parish Registers Index: Caundle Marsh Parish
  www.rootsweb.com/~engdorse/CAUNDLE_MARSH.html
  Brief extracts only

Cerne Abbas
- Dorset Parish Registers Index: Parish of Cerne Abbas Baptisms 1654-1850
  www.rootsweb.com/~engdorse/CERNE_ABBAS.html
  Brief extracts only

- Dorset Parish Registers Index: Parish of Cerne Abbas Marriages 1600-1900
  www.rootsweb.com/~engdorse/CERNE_ABBAS1.html
  Brief extracts only
- Dorset Parish Registers Index: Parish of Cerne Abbas Burials 1701-1750
  www.rootsweb.com/~engdorse/CERNE_ABBAS2.html
  Brief extracts only

Chalbury
- Dorset Parish Registers Index: Chalbury Parish
  www.rootsweb.com/~engdorse/CHALBURY.html
  Brief extracts only

Chardstock
- Dorset Parish Registers Index: Chardstock Parish
  www.rootsweb.com/~engdorse/CHARDSTOCK.html
  Brief extracts only

Charlton Marshall
- Dorset Parish Registers Index: Charlton Marshall Parish
  www.rootsweb.com/~engdorse/CHARLTON_MARSHALL.html
  Brief extracts only

Charminster
- Dorset Parish Registers Index: Charminster Parish Marriages 1590-1690
  www.rootsweb.com/~engdorse/CHARMINSTER.html
  Brief extracts only

Charmouth
- Dorset Parish Registers Index: Charmouth Parish
  www.rootsweb.com/~engdorse/CHARMOUTH.html
  Brief extracts only
- Dorset Parish Registers Index: Charmouth Independent Parish
  www.rootsweb.com/~engdorse/CHARMOUTH_INDEPENDENT.html
  Brief extracts only

Chedington
- Dorset Parish Registers Index: Chedington Parish
  www.rootsweb.com/~engdorse/CHEDINGTON.html
  Brief extracts only

Cheselborne
- Dorset Parish Registers Index: Cheselborne Parish
  www.rootsweb.com/~engdorse/CHESELBORNE.html
  Brief extracts only

Chettle
- Dorset Parish Registers Index: Chettle Parish
  www.rootsweb.com/~engdorse/CHETTLE.html
  Brief extracts only

Chickerell
- Dorset Parish Registers Index: Chickerell Parish
  www.rootsweb.com/~engdorse/CHICKERELL.html
  Brief extracts only

Chideock
- Dorset Parish Registers Index: Chideock Parish
  www.rootsweb.com/~engdorse/CHIDEOCK.html
  Brief extracts only

Chilcombe
- Dorset Parish Registers Index: Chilcombe Parish
  www.rootsweb.com/~engdorse/CHILCOMBE.html
  Brief extracts only

Chilfrome
- Dorset Parish Registers Index: Chilfrome Parish
  www.rootsweb.com/~engdorse/CHILFROME.html
  Brief extracts only

Church Knowle
- Dorset Parish Registers Index: Church Knowle Parish
  www.rootsweb.com/~engdorse/CHURCH_KNOWLE.html
  Brief extracts only

Coombe Keynes
- Dorset Parish Registers Index: Combe Keynes and Wool Parish
  www.rootsweb.com/~engdorse/COMBE_KEYNES_WOOL.html
  Brief extracts only

Compton Abbas
- Dorset Parish Registers Index: Compton Abbas Parish
  www.rootsweb.com/~engdorse/COMPTON_ABBAS.html
  Brief extracts only

Compton Valence
- Dorset Parish Registers Index: Compton Valence Parish
  www.rootsweb.com/~engdorse/COMPTON_VALENCE.html
  Brief extracts only

Corfe Castle
- Dorset Parish Registers Index: Parish of Corfe Castle
  www.rootsweb.com/~engdorse/CORFE_CASTLE.html
  Brief extracts only

Corfe Mullen
- Dorset Parish Registers Index: Corfe Mullen Parish: Parish of Corfe Mullen Baptisms 1800-1900
  www.rootsweb.com/~engdorse/CORFE_MULLEN.html
  Brief extracts only

- Dorset Parish Registers Index: Corfe Mullen Parish: Parish of Corfe Mullen Marriages 1650-1900
  www.rootsweb.com/~engdorse/CORFE_MULLEN1.html
  Brief extracts only

Corscombe
- Dorset Parish Registers Index: Corscombe Parish
  www.rootsweb.com/~engdorse/CORSCOMBE.html
  Brief extracts

Cranborne
- Dorset Parish Registers Index: Cranborne Parish
  www.rootsweb.com/~engdorse/CRANBORNE.html
  Brief extracts only

Dewlish
- Dorset Parish Registers Index: Dewlish Parish
  www.rootsweb.com/~engdorse/DEWLISH.html
  Brief extracts only

Dorchester
- Dorset Parish Registers Index: All Saints Parish of Dorchester: All Saints Dorchester Baptisms 1750-1850
  www.rootsweb.com/~engdorse/DORCHESTER_ALL_SAINTS.html
  Brief extracts only

- Dorset Parish Registers Index: Holy Trinity Parish of Dorchester: Holy Trinity Dorchester Baptisms 1790-1900
  www.rootsweb.com/~engdorse/DORCHESTER_HOLY_TRINITY.html
  Brief extracts only

- Dorset Parish Registers Index: St. Peter's Parish of Dorchester: St. Peter's Dorchester: Baptisms 1800-1900
  www.rootsweb.com/~engdorse/DORCHESTER_ST._PETER'S.html
  Brief extracts only

Durweston
- Dorset Parish Registers Index: Durweston Parish
  www.rootsweb.com/~engdorse/DURWESTON.html
  Brief extracts only

East Chelborough
- Dorset Parish Registers Index: East Chelborough Parish
  www.rootsweb.com/~engdorse/EAST_CHELBOROUGH.html
  Brief extracts only

East Stoke
- Dorset Parish Registers Index: East Stoke Parish: Parish of East Stoke Marriages 1700-1900
  www.rootsweb.com/~engdorse/EAST_STOKE.html
  Brief extracts only

- Dorset Parish Registers Index: East Stoke Parish: East Stoke Burials 1700-1900
  www.rootsweb.com/~engdorse/EAST_STOKE1.html
  Brief extracts only

Edmundsham
- Dorset Parish Registers Index: Edmundsham Parish
  www.rootsweb.com/~engdorse/EDMUNDSHAM.html
  Brief extracts only

Evershot
- Dorset Parish Registers Index: Evershot Parish
  www.rootsweb.com/~engdorse/EVERSHOT.html
  Brief extracts only

Fifehead Magdalen
- Dorset Parish Registers Index: Fifehead Magdalen Parish
  www.rootsweb.com/~engdorse/FIFEHEAD__MAGDALEN.html>
  Brief extracts only

Fifehead Neville
- Dorset Parish Registers Index: Fifehead Neville Parish
  www.rootsweb.com/~engdorse/FIFEHEAD__NEVILLE.html
  Brief extracts only

Fleet
- Dorset Parish Registers Index: Fleet Parish
  www.rootsweb.com/~engdorse/FLEET.html
  Brief extracts only

Folke
- Dorset Parish Registers Index: Parish of Folke Baptisms 1800-1900
  www.rootsweb.com/~engdorse/FOLKE.html
  Brief extracts only

- Dorset Parish Registers Index: Folke Marriages 1800-1895
  www.rootsweb.com/≈engdorse/FOLKE1.html
  Brief extracts only

- Dorset Parish Registers Index: Folke Parish: Parish of Folke Burials, 1800-1895
  www.rootsweb.com/~engdorse/FOLKE2.html
  Brief extracts only

Fontmell Magna
- Dorset Parish Registers Index: Fontmell Magna Parish
  www.rootsweb.com/~engdorse/FONTMELL__MAGNA.html
  Brief extracts only

Fordington
- Dorset Parish Registers Index: Fordington Parish
  www.rootsweb.com/~engdorse/FORDINGTON.html
  Brief extracts only

Fortuneswell
- Dorset Parish Registers Index: Fortuneswell Parish
  www.rootsweb.com/~engdorse/FORTUNESWELL.html
  Brief extracts only

Frampton
- Dorset Parish Registers Index: Frampton Parish
  www.rootsweb.com/~engdorse/FRAMPTON.html
  Brief extracts only

Frome Billett
- Dorset Parish Registers Index: Frome Billett Parish
  www.rootsweb.com/~engdorse/FROME__BILLETT.html
  Brief extracts only

Frome Vauchurch
- Dorset Parish Registers Index: Frome Vauchurch Parish
  www.rootsweb.com/~engdorse/FROME__VAUCHURCH.html
  Brief extracts only

Goathill
- Dorset Parish Registers Index: Goathill Parish
  www.rootsweb.com/~engdorse/GOATHILL.html
  Brief extracts only

- Dorset Parish Registers Index: Godmanstone Baptisms 1800-1900
  www.rootsweb.com/~engdorse/GODMANSTONE.html
  Brief extracts only

Grimstone
- Dorset Parish Registers Index: Grimstone Parish
  www.rootsweb.com/~engdorse/GRIMSTONE.html
  Brief extracts only

Gussage
- Dorset Parish Registers Index: Gussage All Saints Church
  www.rootsweb.com/~engdorse/GUSSAGE__ALL__SAINTS.html
  Brief extracts only

- Dorset Parish Registers Index: Gussage St Michael Parish
  www.rootsweb.com/~engdorse/GUSSAGE__ST__MICHAEL.html
  Brief extracts only

Halstock
- Dorset Parish Registers Index: Halstock Parish
  www.rootsweb.com/~engdorse/HALSTOCK.html
  Brief extracts only

Hammoon
- Dorset Parish Registers Index: Hammoon Parish
  www.rootsweb.com/~engdorse/HAMMOON.html
  Brief extracts only

Hampreston
- Dorset Parish Registers Index: Hampreston Parish
  www.rootsweb.com/~engdorse/HAMPRESTON.html
  Brief extracts only

Hanford
- Dorset Parish Registers Index: Hanford Parish
  www.rootsweb.com/~engdorse/HANFORD.html
  Brief extracts only

Hawkchurch
- Dorset Parish Registers Index: Hawkchurch Parish
  www.rootsweb.com/~engdorse/HAWKCHURCH.html
  Brief extracts only

Haydon
- Dorset Parish Registers Index: Haydon Parish
  www.rootsweb.com/~engdorse/HAYDON.html
  Brief extracts only

Hilton
- Dorset Parish Registers Index: Hilton Parish: Parish of Hilton Burials 1800-1895
  www.rootsweb.com/~engdorse/HILTON.html
  Brief extracts only

Loders
- Dorset Parish Registers Index: Parish of Loders: Loders Parish Register Baptisms 1790-1890
  www.rootsweb.com/~engdorse/LODERS.html
  Brief extracts only

Milton Abbas
- Dorset Parish Registers Index: Milton Abbas Parish: Milton Abbas Baptisms 1800-1915
  www.rootsweb.com/~engdorse/MILTON__ABBAS.html
  Brief extracts only

- Dorset Parish Registers Index: Milton Abbas Parish: Milton Abbas Marriages
  www.rootsweb.com/~engdorse/MILTON__ABBAS1.html
  Brief extracts only

- Dorset Parish Registers Index: Milton Abbas Parish
  www.rootsweb.com/~engdorse/MILTON__ABBAS2.html
  Burials 1738-1895; brief extracts only

Motcombe
- Dorset Parish Registers Index: Motcombe Baptisms 1676-1800
  www.rootsweb.com/~engdorse/MOTCOMBE.html
  Brief extracts only

Netherbury
- Dorset Parish Registers Index: Netherbury Parish: Parish of Netherbury Baptisms 1813-1823
  www.rootsweb.com/~engdorse/NETHERBURY.html
  Brief extracts only, continued as follows:
  1824-1840 /NETHERBURY1.html
  1841-1860 /NETHERBURY2.html
  1861-1880 /NETHERBURY3.html

Nether Compton
- Dorset Parish registers Index: Parish of Nether Compton: Baptisms 1600-1895
  www.rootsweb.com/~engdorse/NETHER__COMPTON.html
  Brief extracts only

- Dorset Parish Registers Index: Nether Compton Parish
  www.rootsweb.com/~engdorse/NETHER__COMPTON1.html
  Marriages 1600-1895; brief extracts only

- Dorset Parish Registers Index: Nether Compton Parish
  www.rootsweb.com/~engdorse/NETHER__COMPTON2.html
  Burials 1600-1895; brief extracts only

- Dorset Parish Registers Index: Parish of North Wootton
  www.rootsweb.com/~engdorse/NORTH__WOOTTON.html
  Brief extracts only

Oborne
- Dorset Parish Registers Index: Oborne Baptisms 1568-1812
  www.rootsweb.com/~engdorse/OBORNE.html
  Brief extracts only

Over Compton
- Dorset Parish Registers Index: Over Compton Parish
  www.rootsweb.com/~engdorse/OVER__COMPTON.html
  Baptisms 1700-1850; Brief extracts only

- Dorset Parish Registers Index: Over Compton Parish; Over Compton Burials 1700-1850
  www.rootsweb.com/~engdorse/OVER__COMPTON1.html
  Brief extracts only

Piddletown
- Dorset Parish Registers Index: Parish of Piddletown also known Puddletown
  www.rootsweb.com/~engdorse/PIDDLETOWN.html
  Brief extracts only

Pimperne
- Dorset Parish Registers Index: Pimperne Parish: Pimperne Baptisms 1800-1900
  www.rootsweb.com/~engdorse/PIMPERNE.html
  Brief extracts only

- Dorset Parish Registers Index: Parish of Pimperne Marriages 1700-1900
  www.rootsweb.com/~engdorse/PIMPERNE1.html
  Brief extracts only

Poole
- Dorset Parish Registers Index: Poole Parish; Poole Marriages 1700-1900
  www.rootsweb.com/~engdorse/POOLE.html
  Brief extracts only

Portland
- Dorset Parish Registers Index: Parish of Portland
  www.rootsweb.com/~engdorse/PORTLAND.html
  Brief extracts only

- Index for the Portland Cemeteries, Dorset
  members.netscapeonline.co.uk/pbtyc/Mls/MI__Index.html
  Index to register

Pulham
- Pulham Marriages 1731 to 1844 (Bishops' transcripts)
  www.westcountrygenealogy.com/blackmore/pulham/marriages.htm

Puncknowle
- Dorset Parish Registers Index: Puncknowle Parish Marriages 1732-1800
  www.rootsweb.com/~engdorse/PUNCKNOWLE5.html
  Brief extracts only

Rampisham
- Dorset Parish Registers Index: Rampisham Parish
  www.rootsweb.com/~engdorse/RAMPISHAM.html
  Baptisms 1800-1850; brief extracts only

Sandford Orcas
- Dorset Parish Registers Index: Sandford Orcas Parish; Parish of Sandford Orcas Baptisms 1700-1895
  www.rootsweb.com/~engdorse/SANDFORD__ORCAS.html
  Brief extracts only

- Dorset Parish Registers Index: Sandford Orcas Parish; Sandford Orcas Burials 1700-1850
  www.rootsweb.com/~engdorse/SANDFORD__ORCAS1.html
  Brief extracts only

Shaftesbury
- Dorset Parish Registers Index: Shaftsbury-St James Parish Register
  www.rootsweb.com/~engdorse/SHAFTSBURY__ST__JAMES.html
  Baptisms 1676-1700; brief extracts only. Continued to 1750 at
  /SHAFTSBURY__ST__JAMES1.html

- Dorset Parish Registers Index: Primitive Methodist Circuit of Shaftsbury
  www.rootsweb.com/~engdorse/
                 SHAFTSBURY__PRIMITIVE__METHODIST.html
  Brief extracts only

Shapwick

- Dorset Parish Registers Index: Parish of Shapwick Baptisms 1600-1895
  www.rootsweb.com/~engdorse/SHAPWICK.html
  Brief extracts only

- Dorset Parish Registers Index: Shapwick Marriages 1700-1900
  www.rootsweb.com/~engdorse/SHAPWICK1.html
  Brief extracts only

Sherborne

- Dorset Parish Registers Index: Parish of Sherborne
  www.rootsweb.com/~engdorse/SHERBORNE.html
  Baptisms 1700-1850; brief extracts only

- Dorset Parish Registers Index: Parish of Sherborne: Sherborne Marriages 1700-1900
  www.rootsweb.com/~engdorse/SHERBORNE1.html
  Brief extracts only

- Dorset Parish Registers Index: Sherborne Parish: Sherborne Burials 1700-1905
  www.rootsweb.com/~engdorse/SHERBORNE2.html
  Brief extracts only

Stalbridge

- Stalbridge: Marriages 1738 to 1847 (Bishops' transcripts)
  www.westcountrygenealogy.com/blackmore/stalbridge/marriages.htm

Stoke Abbott

- Dorset Parish Registers Index: Stoke Abbott Parish
  www.rootsweb.com/~engdorse/STOKE__ABBOTT.html
  Baptisms 1800-1850; brief extracts only

- Dorset Parish Registers Index: Stoke Abbott Parish; Stoke Abbott Marriages 1700-1850
  www.rootsweb.com/~engdorse/STOKE__ABBOTT1.html
  Brief extracts only

Sturminster Marshall

- Dorset Parish Registers Index: Sturminster Marshall Parish: Sturminster Marshall Baptisms 1700-1850
  www.rootsweb.com/~engdorse/STURMINSTER__MARSHALL.html
  Brief extracts only

- Dorset Parish Registers Index: Sturminster Marshall Parish: Sturminster Marshall Marriages 1600-1850
  www.rootsweb.com/~engdorse/STURMINSTER__MARSHALL1.html
  Brief extracts only

- Dorset Parish Registers Index: Sturminster Marshall Parish: Sturminster Marshall Burials 1700-1905
  www.rootsweb.com/~engdorse/STURMINSTER__MARSHALL2.html
  Brief extracts only

Sturminster Newton

- Sturminster Newton Marriages 1731 to 1805 (Bishops' transcripts)
  www.westcountrygenealogy.com/sturminster__newton/marriages.htm

Symondsbury

- Dorset Parish Registers Index: Symondsbury Parish: Symondsbury Baptisms 1800-1900
  www.rootsweb.com/~engdorse/SYMONDSBURY.html
  Brief extracts only

Thorncombe

- Dorset Parish Registers Index: Parish of Thorncombe
  www.rootsweb.com/~engdorse/THORNCOMBE.html
  Brief extracts only

Tolpuddle

- Dorset Parish Registers Index: Tolpuddle Parish Baptisms 1800-1880
  www.rootsweb.com/~engdorse/TOLPUDDLE.html
  Brief extracts only

- Dorset Parish Registers Index: Tolpuddle Parish: Tolpuddle Marriages 1700-1850
  www.rootsweb.com/~engdorse/TOLPUDDLE1.html
  Brief extracts only

- Dorset Parish Registers Index: Tolpuddle Parish: Tolpuddle Burials 1828-1829
  www.rootsweb.com/~engdorse/TOLPUDDLE2.html
  Brief extracts only

Walditch
- Dorset Parish Registers Index: Parish of Walditch: Walditch Baptisms 1740-1870
  www.rootsweb.com/~engdorse/WALDITCH.html
  Brief extracts only

- Dorset Parish Registers Index: Parish of Walditch Marriages 1700-1900
  www.rootsweb.com/~engdorse/WALDITCH1.html
  Brief extracts only

- Dorset Parish Registers Index: Parish of Walditch Burials 1700-1900
  www.rootsweb.com/~engdorse/WALDITCH2.html
  Brief extracts only

Whitchurch Canonicorum
- Dorset Parish Registers Index: Whitchurch Canonicorum: Whitchurch Canonicorum Baptisms 1558-1812
  www.rootsweb.com/~engdorse/WHITCHURCH__CANONICORUM.html

Wool
See Coombe Keynes

Gloucestershire and Bristol

Civil Registration
- Registration Districts in Gloucestershire
  www.fhsc.org.uk/genuki/reg/gls.htm
  Between 1837 and 1930 (including Bristol)

- [St.Catherine's House Marriage Index, Jan-March, 1849. District 11. Gloucestershire *etc.*]
  www.cs.ncl.ac.uk/genuki/StCathsTranscriptions/CATH4911.TXT

Parish & Non-Parochial Registers: Introductory Pages & Lists
- Parish Records
  archives.gloscc.gov.uk/dservea/index.htm
  Registers *etc.* held by Gloucestershire Record Office

- Gloucestershire
  www.sog.org.uk/prc/gloucester.html
  Parish registers, printed, typescript, *etc.,* in the library of the Society of Genealogists

- Quaker Family History Society: Gloucestershire
  www.rootsweb.com/~engqfhs/Research/counties/gloucs.htm
  Notes on Quaker records

Indexes
- Samples of the Gloucestershire Marriage Index
  www.cix.co.uk/~rd/GENUKI/marindex.htm
  Offline searches available

- The Gloucestershire Record Office Genealogical Database
  www.gloscc.gov.uk/pubserv/gcc/corpserv/archives/genealogy.htm
  Includes non-conformist baptisms

- Gloucestershire Burial Index
  www.cix.co.uk/~rd/GENUKI/gbi.htm
  Details of an index on CD; covers c.1813-51.

- Sample of the Gloucestershire misc.strays index
  www.cix.co.uk/~rd/GENUKI/strays.htm
  Including extracts from registers *etc.*

- Extracts from Gloucestershire Church Records
  www.genuki.org.uk/big/eng/GLS/GLSMarriages/
  Marriage index
- IGI Batch Numbers: Gloucestershire Batch Numbers
  freepages.genealogy.rootsweb.com/~tyeroots/glou.html
- IGI Batch Numbers for Gloucester (A-M), England
  freepages.genealogy.rootsweb.com/~hughwallis/IGIBatchNumbers/
  CountyGloucester__(A-M).htm
  Continued at /CountyGloucester__(N-Z).htm
- A Surname index to Online Transcriptions from Phillimore's Gloucestershire
  www.genuki.org.uk/big/eng/GLS/StuartFlight/index.html

Transcript Collections on the Web
- Gloucestershire Parishes
  web.ukonline.co.uk/flight/parish.html
  Many pages of parish register transcripts, *etc.*, separately listed below

Abinghall
- Abenhall
  www.neep.demon.co.uk/fhist/gls-fod/parish/abenhall.html
  Includes marriages 1778-1812, burials 1791-1808. In progress.
- Parish of Abenhall: Burials 1778-1812
  www.neep.demon.co.uk/dean/abenhall/burials.html

Alvington
- Alvington
  www.neep.demon.co.uk/fhist/gls-fod/parish/alvington.html
  Brief list of registers *etc.*

Arlingham
- Arlingham, Gloucestershire Parish Register Notes
  web.ukonline.co.uk/flight/arlingham.html
  From *Gloucestershire notes & queries* **1**, 1881.

Blockley
- Blockley Baptisms 1538-1612
  www.allthecotswolds.com
  Click on 'site map' and title. Continued to 1812 on 4 further pages

- Blockley Parish Marriages 1539-1630
  members.shaw.ca/panthers2/BlockMars1539to1630.html
  Continued to 1978 on 4 further pages
- Blockley Burials 1538-1630
  members.shaw.ca/panthers1/BlockBurials1538to1630.html
  Continued to 1812 on 3 further pages

Brimpsfield
- Brimpsfield, Gloucestershire. Extracts from Parish Registers
  web.ukonline.co.uk/flight/brimpsfieldpr.html
  Extracts for 1591-1806 from *Gloucestershire Notes & Queries* **1**.

Bristol
- Bristol Marriage Bonds and Allegations, 1679 (regretfully incomplete)
  www.genuki.org.uk/big/eng/GLS/Bristol/MarriageBonds1679.html
  From *Gloucestershire notes & queries* **10**, 1914
- Badcox Lane Baptist Church Records
  www.gomezsmarts.free-online.co.uk
  In Bristol, c.1734-1807. Names only, no dates. Click on __Churches__ and title

Cam
- Marriages at Cam, Gloucestershire 1569 to 1812
  www.genuki.org.uk/big/eng/GLS/Cam/camstart.html
  Extracted from the Phillimore transcription

Charlton Kings
- Charlton Kings, Gloucestershire Parish Registers, Marriages, 1538-1811
  web.ukonline.co.uk/flight/charlton.html
  Originally published in *Gloucestershire notes & queries* **4**, 1890

Chedworth
- Marriages: St. Andrew's Church, Chedworth, 1837-1851
  members.shaw.ca/panthers2/ChadworthStAndrewsMarr.html
- Baptisms at Chedworth Congregational Chapel 1841-1855
  members.shaw.ca/panthers2/ChedworthCongregational.html

Chipping Campden
- Chipping Campden Marriage Registers
  members.shaw.ca/panthers3/ChippingMarRegisters.html
  Covers 1717-1837

- Chipping Campden Baptisms Marriages & Burials
  members.shaw.ca/panthers2/ChipBurMarBapt.html
  Extracts from a book published 1911

Cinderford
- Cinderford
  www.neep.demon.co.uk/fhist/glo-fod/parish/cinderford.html
  List of registers, *etc.*

Coaley
- Coaley, Gloucestershire Parish Registers: Extracts of Births, Marriages & Deaths
  web.ukonline.co.uk/flight/coaley.html
  From *Gloucestershire Notes & Queries* **4**, 1890

Coleford
- Coleford
  www.neep.demon.co.uk/fhist/glo-fod/parish/coleford.html
  List of registers

Cromhall
- Cromhall Bishops' transcripts, Gloucestershire, 1571 to 1640
  www.genuki.org.uk/big/eng/GLS/Cromhall/CromhallBTs.html

Didmarton
- Didmarton, Gloucestershire Marriages 1675-1751
  web.ukonline.co.uk/flight/didmartonmar.html
  hometown.aol.com/k2m3/didmartmarr01.html
  From the Phillimore transcription

- Didmarton & Oldbury on the Hill Marriages (Gloucestershire) 1754-1812
  hometown.aol.com/k2m3/didmartmarr02.html
  See also Oldbury on the Hill

Eastcombe
- Eastcombe Marriages 1837-1865
  www.genuki.org.uk/big/eng/GLS/Eastcombe/eastm1.html
  Continued to 1952 on 4 further pages

- Marriages at Eastcombe Baptist Church, Gloucestershire, UK 1837-1952
  www.genuki.org.uk/big/eng/GLS/Eastcombe/Eastc-mars.html

- Eastcombe Burials 1806-1876
  www.genuki.org.uk/big/eng/GLS/Eastcombe/eastb1.html
  Continued to 1970 on 3 further pages

- Burials at Eastcombe Baptist Church, Gloucestershire, UK, 1806-1970
  www.genuki.org.uk/eng/GLS/Eastcombe/Eastc-burs.html

Forest of Dean
- Royal Forest of Dean Family History: Parish Registers and Non-Conformist Chapel Records, Village Records, *etc.*
  www.neep.demon.co.uk/fhist/gls-fod/parishes.html
  Collection of parish register lists and transcripts *etc.*, some separately listed here.

Frocester
- Frocester Marriages 1559-1565
  hometown.aol.com/K2m3/frocest.html
  Continued to 1613 on 4 further pages

- Frocester Parish Registers: Marriages 1559-1800
  www.geocities.com/Heartland/Ranch/8066/frocest.html
  Originally published in *Gloucestershire notes and queries* **5**, 1891-3.

Great Rissington
- Marriages at Great Rissington, Gloucestershire, 1538-1913
  www.genuki.org.uk/big/eng/GLS/GreatRissington/grstart.html
  From the Phillimore transcription

Hawkesbury
- Hawkesbury, Gloucestershire, Extracts from Parish Registers, Births, Marriages & Deaths
  www.geocities.com/Heartland/Ranch/8066/hawkreg.html
  web.ukonline.co.uk/flight/hawkreg.html
  Originally published in *Gloucestershire Notes & Queries* **5**, 1894

- Hawkesbury and Hillesley Family History
  www.hawkesburyfamilyhistory.co.uk/
  The 'private' pages include a transcript of Hawkesbury burial register, 1786-1884, accessible for a fee

Hillesley
See Hawkesbury

King's Stanley
- King's Stanley, Gloucestershire Parish Registers: Marriages 1573-1812
  web.ukonline.co.uk/flight/stanley/ksstart.html
  From the Phillimore transcription

Lydney
- Lydney
  www.neep.demon.co.uk/fhist/glo-fod/parish/lydney.html
  List of registers

Maisemore
- Maisemore Parish Registers: Births Marriages & Deaths
  www.geocities.com/Heartland/Ranch/8066/maisereg.html
  web.ukonline.co.uk/flight/maisereg.html
  From *Gloucestershire Notes & Queries* **4**, 1890

Minchinhampton
- Parish Registers 1566-1812: Minchinhampton
  web.ukonline.co.uk/flight/minchin/index.html
  From the Phillimore transcription. In progress

- Minchinhampton Marriages 1566-1702 and Church Monuments
  www.grahamthomas.com/Minchmarr1.html
  From the Phillimore transcription

Mitcheldean
- Parish of Mitcheldean, Gloucestershire: Marriages 1680-1812
  www2.tpg.com.au/users/dsteel/marmitch.htm

North Nibley
- Baptisms at North Nibley Congregational Tabernacle, Gloucestershire, U.K., 1826-1850
  www.genuki.org.uk/big/eng/GLS/NorthNibley/NNTabBapt.html
  Continued to 1906 at **/NNTabBapt2.html**

- Burials at North Nibley Congregational Tabernacle, Gloucestershire, U.K., 1863-1895
  www.genuki.org.uk/big/eng/GLS/NorthNibley/NNTabBur.html

Nympsfield
- Marriages at Nimpsfield: 1679-1756 & Census 1851
  www.grahamthomas.com/Nimpsfield1.html

- Marriages at Nympsfield, Glos., 1679-1753
  web.ukonline.co.uk/flight.nympmar1.html
  Originally published in *Gloucestershire notes & queries* **6**, 1894-5.
  Continued to 1810 at **/nympmar2.html**

Oldbury on the Hill
- Oldbury on the Hill, Gloucestershire, UK: Marriages 1568-1751
  web.ukonline.co.uk/flight/oldburyonhillmar.html
  From the Phillimore transcription

- Marriage Register of parishes of Oldbury-on-the-Hill & Didmarton, Gloucestershire, UK 1754-1812
  web.ukonline.co.uk/flight/oldburydidmar.html
  From the Phillimore transcription
  See also Didmarton

Olveston
- Olveston Parish Register 1741-1812 (extracts)
  www.genuki.org.uk/big/eng/GLS/Olveston/PPNotes.html
  Brief notes with a few extracts

Owlpen
- Marriages at Owlpen, Glos., 1687-1837
  web.ukonline.co.uk/flight/owlpen.html
  From *Gloucestershire notes & queries* **6**, 1894-5.

Quedgeley
- Marriages at Quedgeley, Glos., 1559-1836
  web.ukonline.co.uk/flight/quedgeley.html
  From the Phillimore transcription

Quenington
- Baptisms at Quenington, Gloucestershire, 1841 to 1891
  www.genuki.org.uk/big/eng/GLS/Quenington/Baptisms1841to1891.html

- Marriages at Quenington, Gloucestershire, 1841 to 1891
  www.genuki.org.uk/big/eng/GLS/Quenington/Marriages1841to1891.html

Randwick
- Randwick, Gloucestershire
  www.sandford.plus.com/Randwick/index.html
  Baptism 1762-1812; banns 1770-1812; marriages 1762-1836; burials 1762-1812, *etc.,*

Rangeworthy
- Rangeworthy Bishops' transcripts 1575 to 1640
  www.genuki.org.uk/big/eng/GLS/Rangeworthy/RangeworthyBTs.html

Ruardean
- Ruardean
  www.neep.demon.co.uk/fhist/gls-fod/parish/ruardean.html
  List of registers and transcripts

Sevenhampton
- Sevenhampton Burials 1750-1799
  members.shaw.ca/panthers2/SevenhamptonBurials1750.html
  Continued for 1800-1850 at **/SevenhamptonBurials1800.html**

Slimbridge
- Slimbridge, Gloucestershire Marriages 1635-1812
  web.ukonline.co.uk/flight/slimbridge.html
  From the Phillimore transcription

Stroud
- Stroud Area, Gloucestershire
  web.ukonline.co.uk/flight/stroudarea.html
  Brief extracts from various parish registers, *etc.*

Tetbury
- Tetbury, Gloucestershire Burial Registers
  web.ukonline.co.uk/flight/tetburyprburial.html
  Extracts, 1631-1811

Uley
- Uley, Gloucestershire: Extracts from Parish Registers
  web.ukonline.co.uk/flight/uleyreg.html
  From the Phillimore transcription

Westbury on Severn
- Annotated Burials at Westbury on Severn, 1889-1895
  www.rebus.demon.co.uk/wos__br.htm

Whaddon
- Whaddon Parish Register; Births, Marriages & Deaths 1674-1711
  web.ukonline.co.uk/flight/whadreg.html
  From *Gloucestershire Notes & Queries* **4**, 1890

Winchcombe
- Winchcombe: Index to Phillimore's Marriages 1539-1812
  pages.britishlibrary.net/winchcombe/phillmar.htm

Woolaston
- Woolaston
  www.neep.demon.co.uk/fhist/glo-fod/parish/worlaston.html
  List of registers

Hampshire

Civil Registration
- Registration Districts in Hampshire
  www.fhsc.org.uk/genuki/reg/ham.htm
  Between 1837 and 1930

- Civil Registration
  website.lineone.net/~hantshistory/civil.html
  List of sites for Hampshire

- The Register Offices of Hampshire
  www.hants.gov.uk/regulatory/registra/offices.html
  Addresses

- Registration Districts in Hampshire
  www.fhsc.org.uk/genuki/reg/ham.htm
  From 1837 to 1930

- [St. Catherine's House Marriage Index, Jan-March, 1849. District 7. Hampshire/Sussex]
  www.cs.ncl.ac.uk/genuki/StCathsTranscriptions/CATH4907.TXT

Parish & Non-Parochial Registers: Introductory Pages & Lists
See also Devon

- Hampshire & Isle of Wight
  www.sog.org.uk/prc/hampshire.html
  Parish registers, printed, typescripts, *etc.,* in the library of the Society of Genealogists

- Parish Registers
  www.iow.gov.uk/library/record__office/Types__of__Records/parishre.asp
  Held by the Isle of Wight Record Office

- Parish Registers
  website.lineone.net/~hantshistory.pr.html
  Details and index of Phillimore transcriptions, various transcripts, publications, *etc.*

Indexes
- Free Reg: Hampshire
  freereg.rootsweb.com/parishes/ham/index.htm
  Details of the registers currently included in the project to index births, deaths, and marriages.

- IGI Batch Numbers: Hampshire Batch Numbers
  freepages.genealogy.rootsweb.com/~tyeroots/hampshire.html

- IGI Batch Numbers for Hampshire, England
  freepages.genealogy.rootsweb.com/~hughwallis/IGIBatchNumbers/County Hampshire.htm

- Hampshire, England: Parish and Probate Records
  www.ancestry.com/search/locality/main.htm?uk
  Click on 'England' and 'Hampshire'
  Index to published registers, *etc.*

Publications
- Hampshire Genealogical Society Burial Index 1400-1837, for all Hampshire excluding the Isle of Wight
  www.hgs-online.org.uk/hgs__publications__cd.htm
  Details of a CD

- Parish Register Transcription Society
  www.prtsoc.org.uk
  Lists some published Hampshire Registers

Newspaper Indexes
- Modern Newspaper Index: Hampshire and Surrey Collection
  www.dreamwater.net/anglersrest/surreyhants.htm
  Index of death notices *etc.*

Avington
- St. Mary the Virgin, Avington: Burial Record 1900-1991
  freepages.genealogy.rootsweb.com/~villages/avinburi.htm

Basingstoke
- Phillimore Hampshire Parish Records volume 5
  homepages.rootsweb.com/~mwi/Marr5__b.txt
  Probably relates to Basingstoke, although the web-page does not say so

Bentworth
- Phillimore Parish Records, volume 11: Bentworth banns Published
  homepages.rootsweb.com/~mwi/banns11.txt

Blendworth
- Parish Register Transcripts of Blendworth, Hampshire, UK
  www3.sympatico.ca/jeanearl/Parish2.html
  Index to burials, 19th c., and to baptisms 1813-99.
- Blendworth Burials 1813-1899
  freepages.genealogy.rootsweb.com/~parishregisters/hampshire/ blendworth/Blendworth__Burials__1813-1899.htm
- The Parish of Blendworth
  www.parishregisters.co.uk/
  Click on 'Hampshire' and 'Blendworth'. Burials 1813-1899

Botley
- Botley, Hampshire, Parish Registers
  www.mcportsmouth.freeserve.co.uk/bot/bot.htm
  Covers 1679-1837

Bramshaw
- Bramshaw 1592-1835
  www.wis.mcmail.com/Bramshaw.htm
  Surnames only from the parish register

Colemore
- The Parish of Colemore
  www.parishregisters.co.uk
  Click on 'Hampshire' and 'Colemore'. Baptisms 1563-1975; marriages 1563-1967; burials 1563-1975. Many pages. Also available at
  freepages.genealogy.rootsweb.com/~parishregisters/hampshire/ colemore/colemore.htm

East Meon
- Parish Register Transcripts of East Meon & Langrish, Hampshire, UK
  www.safari.freeserve.co.uk/registers.html
  East Meon baptisms 1560-1899; marriages 1677-1904; burials 1677-1898; Langrish baptisms 1871-1934; marriages 1872-1976.
- Parish Register Transcript of East Meon, Hampshire, UK
  www.parishregisters.co.uk/
  Click on 'Hampshire' and 'East Meon'. In progress. Many pages
  Also at
  freepages.genealogy.rootsweb.com/~parishregisters/ hampshire/eastmeon/eastmeon.htm

Froyle
- Froyle Church and Parish Registers
  www.froyle.demon.co.uk/histnotes4.htm
  General discussion with some extracts

Headley
- Headley, Hampshire: Index to Marriages 1695-1812
  website.lineone.net/~hantshistory/mm-h1-1.html
- Burials at All Saints, Headley, 1539 to 1851
  my.genie.co.uk/headleyvillage/burials/burials.htm
  Index

Herriard
- The Parish of Herriard
  www.parishregisters.co.uk
  Click on 'Hampshire' and 'Herriard'. Baptisms 1791-1852; marriages 1754-1872; burials 1793-1862. Also available at
  freepages.genealogy.rootsweb.com/~parishregisters/hampshire/herriard/ herriard.htm

Hythe
- Hythe Baptisms
  www.btinternet.com/~goldingfamily/Baptindex.html
  In progress, mainly 19th c. at present
- Baptisms to Military Families in Hythe
  www.btinternet.com/~goldingfamily/BaptismsMilitary.html
  For 1799, 1813-20, & 1823. In progress.

Kingsclere
- Burials at Kingslere and Kingsclere Woodlands
  website.lineone.net/~hantshistory/bur-kingsclere.html
  For Kingslere, 1869-75; for Kingsclere Woodlands 1881-5

Langrish
See East Meon

Long Sutton
- [Long Sutton, Marriages, 1561-1783]
  homepages.rootsweb.com/~mwi/Marr5__a.txt
  Probably relates to Long Sutton, although the web page does not say so.

Michelmersh
- Index of Baptisms between 1773 and 1889 from the Registers of the Parish Church of St. Mary's, Michelmersh, Romsey
  www.genuki.org.uk/big/eng/HAM/Michelmersh/BapMersh.html

- Index of Marriages between 1813 and 1989 from the Registers of the Parish Church of St. Mary's, Michelmersh, Romsey
  www.genuki.org.uk/big/eng/HAM/Michelmersh/MarMersh.html

- Index of Burials between 1813 and 1989 from the Registers of the Parish Church of St. Mary's, Michelmersh, Romsey
  www.genuki.org.uk/big/eng/HAM/Michelmersh/Burmersh.html

Newton Valence
- The Parish of Newton Valence
  www.parishregisters.co.uk
  Click on 'Hampshire' and 'Newton Valence'. Baptisms 1538-1896; marriages 1538-1979; burials 1538-1992; banns 1754-1957. Many pages; in progress. Also at
  freepages.genealogy.rootsweb.com/~parishregisters/hampshire/newtonva/newtonva.htm

Otterbourne
- Otterbourne, Hampshire: Marriages 1747-1751
  website.lineone.net/~hantshistory/pr-otterbourne.html

Plaitford
- Plaitford 1622-1836
  www.wis.mcmail.com/Plaitford.htm
  Surnames only from the parish register

Priors Dean
- The Parish of Priors Dean
  www.parishregisters.co.uk/
  Click on 'Hampshire' and 'Priors Dean'. Baptisms 1538-1978; marriages 1538-1977; burials 1538-1978. Many pages; in progress. Also at
  freepages.genealogy.rootsweb.com/~parishregisters/hampshire/priorsde/prirosde.htm

Rowner
- The Register Book of Roughner from the year 1590
  www.portsdown.co.uk/parr.htm
  To 1701

Shipton Bellinger
- Shipton Bellinger, Hampshire: Index to Marriages 1780-1812
  website.lineone.net/~hantshistory/pr-shipton.html

Winchester College
- Phillimore's Hampshire Parish Records, volume 11: Baptisms
  homepages.rootsweb.com/~mwi/h11__bap.txt
  From Winchester College, 1726-1861

- Burials, volume 11, Phillimores Parish Records
  homepages.rootsweb.com/~mwi/h11__bur.txt
  For Winchester College. Index to burials, 15-19th c.

Herefordshire

Civil Registration
- Registration Districts in Herefordshire
  www.fhsc.org.uk/genuki/reg/hef.htm
  Between 1837 and 1930

- Registrars of Births, Deaths and Marriages: Herefordshire
  www.rootsweb.com/~ukhfhs/regist.html

Parish & Non-Parochial Registers: Introductory Pages & Lists
- Parishes of Herefordshire
  www.herefordshire-gen.co.uk/parishregisters.htm
  List

- Herefordshire
  www.sog.org.uk/prc/herefordshire.html
  Parish registers, printed, typescript, *etc.,* in the library of the Society of Genealogists

- Quaker Family History Society: Herefordshire
  www.rootsweb.com/~engqfhs/Research/counties/hereford.htm
  Notes on Quaker records

Indexes
- Herefordshire Burial Index 1813-1839
  www.rootsweb.com/~ukhfhs/burial.html
  Details of an off-line index

- Free Reg: Herefordshire
  freereg.rootsweb.com/parishes/hef/index.htm
  Details of the registers currently included in the project to index births, deaths and marriages

- IGI Batch Numbers: Herefordshire Batch Numbers
  freepages.genealogy.rootsweb.com/~tyeroots/hereford.html

- IGI Batch Numbers for Hereford, England
  freepages.genealogy.rootsweb.com/~hughwallis/IGIBatchNumbers/CountyHereford.htm

Ashperton
- Steve Karners HEF Parish Extracts: Ashperton
  homepages.rootsweb.com/~slkarner/HEF_Parish/HEF_Events_Ashperton.html
  For 1604-5 & 1759-1871

Avenbury
- Steve Karner's HEF Parish Extracts: Avenbury
  homepages.rootsweb.com/~slkarner/HEF_Parish/HEF_Events_Avenbury.html
  Brief extracts from the parish registers

Bishops Frome
- The Parish of Bishop's Frome
  www.parishregisters.co.uk/
  Click on 'Herefordshire' and 'Bishop's Frome'. Marriages 1754-1923; burials 1800-1826. Also at
  freepages.genealogy.rootsweb.com/~parishregisters/herefordshire/bishops/bishops.htm

Bishopstone
- Steve Karner's HEF Parish Extracts: Bishopstone
  homepages.rootsweb.com/~slkarner/HEF_Parish/HEF_Events_Bishopstone.html
  Register extracts, 1797-1845

Brinsop
- Steve Karner's HEF Parish Extracts: Brinsop
  homepages.rootsweb.com/~slkarner/HEF_Parish/HEF_Events_Brinsop.html
  Register extracts, 1769-1861

Canon Pyon
- Steve Karner's HEF Parish Extracts: Canon Pyon, 1662-1689
  homepages.rootsweb.com/~slkarner/HEF_Parish/HEF_Events_CanonPyon1.htm
  Register extracts. Continued to 1843 on 7 further pages

Colwall
- The Parish of Colwall
  www.parishregisters.co.uk
  Click on 'Herefordshire' and 'Colwall'. Baptisms 1723-1896; marriages 1723-1933; burials 1813-1863

Cradley
- Steve Karner's HEF Parish Extracts: Cradley
  homepages.rootsweb.com/~slkarner/HEF__Parish/
  HEF__Events__Cradley.html
  Register extracts, 1768-1865

Eye
- Steve Karner's HEF Parish Extracts: Eye
  homepages.rootsweb.com/~slkarner/HEF__Parish/
  HEF__Events__Eye.html
  Register extracts, 1761-1805

Kingsland
- Steve Karner's HEF Parish Extracts: Kingsland, 1792-1821
  homepages.rootsweb.com/~slkarner/HEF__Parish/
  HEF__Events__Kingsland1.html

- Steve Karner's HEF Parish Extracts: Kingsland, 1822-1950
  homepages.rootsweb.com/~slkarner/HEF__Parish/
  HEF__Events__Kingsland2.html

Kington
- Steve Karner's HEF Parish Extracts: Kington
  homepages.rootsweb.com/~slkarner/HEF__Parish/
  HEF__Events__Kington.html
  Register extracts, 1824-1858

Little Cowarne
- Steve Karner's HEF Parish Extracts: Little Cowarne
  homepages.rootsweb.com/~slkarner/HEF__Parish/
  HEF__Events__LittleCowarne.html
  Register extracts, 1852-1858

Little Hereford
- Steve Karner's HEF Parish Extracts: Little Hereford
  homepages.rootsweb.com/~slkarner/HEF__Parish/
  HEF__Events__LittleHereford.html
  Register extracts, 1819-1828

Much Cowarne
- Steve Karner's HEF Parish Extracts: Much Cowarne, 1761-1857
  homepages.rootsweb.com/~slkarner/HEF__Parish/
  HEF__Events__MuchCowarne1.html
- Steve Karner's HEF Parish Extracts: Much Cowarne, 1865-1904
  homepages.rootsweb.com/~slkarner/
  HEF__Parish/HEF__Events__MuchCowarne2.html
- Steve Karner's HEF Parish Extracts: Much Cowarne, 1905-1937
  homepages.rootsweb.com/~slkarner/HEF__Parish/
  HEF__Events__MuchCowarne3.html

Pencombe
- Steve Karner's HEF Parish Extracts: Pencombe
  homepages.rootsweb.com/~slkarner/HEF__Parish/
  HEF__Events__Pencombe.html
  Register extracts, 1818-1821

Sarnesfield
- The Register of Sarnesfield
  www.uk-genealogy.org.uk/england/Herefordshire/Sarnesfield/
  Sarnesfield.index.html
  Facsimile of edition originally published by the Parish Register Society.

Weobley
- Steve Karner's HEF Parish Extracts: Weobley
  homepages.rootsweb.com/~slkarner/HEF__Parish/
  HEF__Events__Weobley.html
  Register extracts, 1834-1838

Kent

Civil Registration
- Registration Districts in Kent
  www.fhsc.org.uk/genuki/reg/Ken.htm
  Between 1837 and 1930
- Kent Registration Services
  www.kent.gov.uk/sp/Kentregserv/home.html
- [St. Catherine's House Marriage Index, Jan-March, 1849. District 5. Kent *etc.*]
  www.cs.ncl.ac.uk/genuki/StCathsTranscriptions/CATH4905.TXT

Parish & Non-Parochial Registers: Introductory Pages & Lists
- How to find Parish Registers in Kent
  www.kent.gov.uk/e&l/artslib/ARCHIVES/atopicparish.html
- Marriage Banns
  www.kent.gov.uk/e&l/artslib/ARCHIVES/atopicbanns.html
  In Kent
- Parish Records held in microform at Folkestone Library
  www.btinternet.com/~goldingfamily/Parish__records.html
- Lewisham Local Studies and Archives: Parish Registers
  www.lewisham.gov.uk/data/yourarea/data/lsa__pari.htm
  List of registers held
- Kent
  www.sog.org.uk/prc/ken.html
  Parish registers, printed, typescript, *etc.,* in the library of the Society of Genealogists
- Quaker Family History Society: Kent
  www.rootsweb.com/~engqfhs/Research/counties/kent.htm
  Notes on Quaker records

Indexes
- Kent Index Information
  freepages.genealogy.rootsweb.com/~mrawson/info.html
  List of baptism, marriage and burial indexes
- Kent Baptisms; Kent Marriages; Kent Burials
  www.rootsweb.com/%7Eengken/bmd.html
  Indexes
- Kent Baptisms Page
  www.sartorelli.gen.nz/tree/kentbaptisms/index.html
  www.rootsweb.com/~engken/bmd.html
  Index to 20,000 records
- Kent Parishes on LDS Vital Records Index
  freepages.genealogy.rootsweb.com/~mrawson/kentrec.html
- IGI Batch Numbers: Kent Batch Numbers
  freepages.genealogy.rootsweb.com/~tyeroots/kent.html
- IGI Batch Numbers for Kent, England
  freepages.genealogy.rootsweb.com/~hughwallis/IGIBatchNumbers/CountyKent.htm
- Kent Resources: the Ted Wildy Marriage Witness Index
  www.digiserve.com/peter/tw/index.htm

Newspaper Indexes
- Newspaper Index, *Dover Telegraph,* Kent
  freepages.genealogy.rootsweb.com/%7Emrawson/newspaper.html
  For 1839-50, presumably including personal announcements

Publications
- Kent Family History Society: CD-ROM Publications
  www.kfhs.org.uk/public2.htm
  Includes some parish registers
- Kent Family History Society Microfiche Publications Index
  www.kfhs.org.uk/mfiche1.htm
  Includes many parish registers
- North West Kent Family History Society: Society Publications List
  www.nwkfhs.org.uk/PUBLICNS.HTM
  Includes parish registers and microfiche

- Kent Parish Registers on Fiche Published by North West Kent Family History Society
  freepages.genealogy.rootsweb.com/~mrawson/prfiche2.html
- Kent Parish Registers on Fiche published by Kent Family History Society
  freepages.genealogy.rootsweb.com/~mrawson/prfiche1.html
  List

Birchington
- All Saints, Birchington, Kent: Marriages 1754-1812
  users.iclway.co.uk/barrywhite/registers/pr__birch__m.pdf

Buckland
- Parish Registers of Buckland, Kent
  freepages.genealogy.rootsweb.com/~mrawson/buckland.html
  Baptisms 1772-1837; marriages 1755-1818; burials 1813-37

Canterbury
- Index of Canterbury Baptisms 1790-1840
  www.Kentgen.com/canterbury.htm
  Offline index

Chislet
- Chislet Church Records
  users.ox.ac.uk/~malcolm/genuki/big/eng/KEN/Chislet/
  Pages for 16 surnames

Farnborough
- Index to Transcript of Bishops' transcripts for Farnborough, Kent
  freepages.genealogy.rootsweb.com/~ptyc/Den/Farnboro/Mar/Index.html
  Marriages 1813-50

Hythe
- Hythe Marriage Oddments
  www.btinternet.com/~goldingfamily/Marriages.html
  Extracts from the registers, 18-19th c.
- Hythe Burials: oddments
  www.btinternet.com/~goldingfamily/Burials.html
  19th c. extracts from the register

Margate
- St John the Baptist, Margate, Kent; Baptisms 1679-1728
  users.iclway.co.uk/barrywhite/registers/pr__marg__c1.pdf
- St John the Baptist, Margate, Kent; Marriages 1686-1812
  users.iclway.co.uk/barrywhite/registers/pr__marg__m.pdf
- St John the Baptist, Margate, Kent; Burials 1681-1753
  users.iclway.co.uk/barrywhite/registers/pr__marg__b1.pdf
  Continued to 1812 at **pr__marg__b2.pdf**
- St John the Baptist, Margate, Kent; Miscellaneous Entries 1679-1812
  users.iclway.co.uk/barrywhite/registers/pr__marg__x.pdf

Monkton
- St Mary Magdalene, Monkton, Kent; Baptisms 1700-1792
  users.iclway.co.uk/barrywhite/registers/pr__monk__c.pdf
- St Mary Magdalene, Monkton, Kent; Marriages 1700-1753
  users.iclway.co.uk/barrywhite/registers/pr__monk__m.pdf
- St Mary Magdalene, Monkton, Kent; Burials 1700-1792
  users.iclway.co.uk/barrywhite/registers/pr__monk__b.pdf

Otterden
- Burials in Otterden, Kent 1660-6, 1682-1812
  freepages.genealogy.rootsweb.com/~mrawson/otterden.html

Thanet
- Index of Isle of Thanet Baptisms 1780-1840
  www.Kentgen.com/thanet.htm
  Brief note on an off-line index
- Diocese of Canterbury Bonds & Allegations: Marriages by licence of Thanet people 1724 & 1734
  users.iclway.co.uk/barrywhite/people/pt__licence.pdf
- Resources for Family and Local History in Thanet
  users.iclway.co.uk/barrywhite/
  Collection of parish register transcripts each separately listed here

London and Middlesex

General
- How Do I Find a Birth, Death or Marriage in London or Middlesex?
  www.rootsweb.com/~engmdx/faq1.html
  Brief discussion of civil registration and parish registers

Civil Registration
- Registration Districts in London
  www.fhsc.org.uk/genuki/reg/lnd.htm
  Between 1837 and 1930
- Registration Districts in Middlesex
  www.fhsc.org.uk/genuki/reg/mdx.htm
  Between 1837 and 1930
- [St. Catherine's House Marriage Index, Jan-March, 1849. District 1: London]
  www.cs.ncl.ac.uk/genuki/StCathsTranscriptions/CATH4901.TXT
  2 further pages cover districts 2 & 3
- [St. Catherine's House Marriage Index. Vol.2. East London, 1843/Q4]
  www.cs.ncl.ac.uk/genuki/StCathsTranscriptions/CATHPRS1.TXT
- [St. Catherine's House Marriage Index: entries for Islington for 1843/Q3 and Shoreditch for 1886/Q3]
  www.cs.ncl.ac.uk/genuki/StCathsTranscriptions/CATHPRSX.TXT

Parish & Non-Parochial Registers: Introductory Pages & Lists
- Guildhall Library Manuscripts Section: City of London Parish Records
  ihr.sas.ac.uk/gh/parrech.htm
  Currently being revised
- London Generations
  www.cityoflondon.gov.uk/family-research/registerSearchForm.asp
  Database of sources, including parish registers, held at London Metropolitan Archives
- Non-Anglican Register transcripts
  www.cityoflondon.gov.uk/leisure__heritage/
      libraries__archives__museums__galleries/lma/pdf/non__anglican.PDF
  At London Metropolitan Archives
- City of London Churches. Anglican Church (Church of England)
  www.gendocs.demon.co.uk/city-ch.html
  Gives details of availability of parish registers
- Westminster Archives Guide: Chapter 15: Ecclesiastical
  www.westminster.gov.uk/libraries/archives/guide/guide15.cfm
  Includes details of parish registers held
- Westminster Archives Guide Chapter 16: Non-Anglican Religious Bodies
  develop.westminster.gov.uk/libraries/archives/guide/guide16.cfm
  Includes list of registers held
- City of London
  www.sog.org.uk/prc/lnd.html
  Parish registers, printed, typescript, *etc.,* in the library of the Society of Genealogists
- Middlesex
  www.sog.org.uk/prc/mdx.html
  Parish registers, printed, typescript, *etc.,* in the library of the Society of Genealogists
- Quaker Family History Society: London & Middlesex
  www.rootsweb.com/~engqfhs/Research/counties/london.htm
  Notes on Quaker records

Marriage Licences
- Marriage Licence Records (Allegations and Bonds) at Guildhall Library
  ihr.sas.ac.uk/gh/marrlic.htm

Indexes
- The Middlesex Marriages Home Page
  pages.britishlibrary.net/eddie.bennett/Middx/mddx-marriages-home.htm
- The Middlesex Marriages Index
  www.angelfire.com/fl/Sumter/Middlesex.html
  Index of published (presumably Harleian Society) registers
- Middlesex, England, Parish Registers
  www.uk-genealogy.org.uk/england/Middlesex/midsex/index.htm
  Database created from published registers (which ones not stated) 1563-1895

- Pallots Baptism Index for England
  www.ancestry.com/search/rectype/inddbs/5968.htm
  Database of 200,000 records, mainly relating to the Greater London area 1780-1837

- IGI Batch Numbers for London including Middlesex (A-M), England
  freepages.genealogy.rootsweb.com/~hughwallis/IGIBatchNumbers/ CountyLondon__including__Middlesex__(A-M).htm
  Continued at **/CountyLondon__including__Middlesex__(N-Z).htm**

- IGI Batch Numbers: Middlesex Batch Numbers
  freepages.genealogy.rootsweb.com/~tyeroots/middle.html

Chiswick
- Chiswick Marriages
  www.west-middlesex-fhs.org.uk/fwm-indx.html
  Click on title. West Middlesex Family History Society lookup service

Fleet Prison
- Fleet Marriages of Hertfordshire People to 1754
  www.hertsfhs.org.uk/hfphs42.html
  General discussion of Hertfordshire marriages in the Fleet Prison, London

Harlington
- Harlington Parish Registers
  www.west-middlesex-fhs.org.uk/fwm.indx
  Click on title. West Middlesex Family History Society lookup service

Harmondsworth
- Harmondsworth Parish Registers
  www.west-middlesex-fhs.org.uk/fwm-indx
  Click on title. West Middlesex Family History Society lookup service

Hayes
- Hayes, St. Mary's Parish Registers
  www.west-middlesex-fhs.org.uk/fwm-indx.htm
  Click on title. West Middlesex Family History Society lookup service

Hillingdon
- Hillingdon Parish Registers
  www.west-middlesex-fhs.org.uk/fwm-indx.htm
  Click on title. West Middlesex Family History Society lookup service

Isleworth
- Isleworth All Saints Parish Registers
  www.west-middlesex-fhs.org.uk/fwm-indx.htm
  Click on title. West Middlesex Family History Society lookup service

New Brentford
- New Brentford, St. Lawrence register
  www.west-middlesex-fhs.org.uk/fwm-indx.htm
  Click on title. West Middlesex Family History Society lookup service

Teddington
- Teddington Index
  www.west-middlesex-fhs.org.uk/fwm-indx.htm
  Click on title. West Middlesex Family History Society lookup service. The index includes the parish records.

Tottenham
- All Hallows, Tottenham: parish registers 1558-1837
  www.mickbruff.pwp.blueyonder.co.uk/highroad/allhallows/ allhallows__prs.html

Oxfordshire

Civil Registration
- Registration Districts in Oxfordshire
  www.fhsc.org.uk/genuki/reg/oxf.htm
  Between 1837 and 1930

- [St. Catherine's House Marriage Index, Jan-March, 1849. District 16. Oxfordshire/Warwickshire]
  www.cs.ncl.ac.uk/genuki/StCathsTranscriptionS/CATH4916.TXT

Parish & Non-Parochial Registers: Introductory Pages & Lists
- Oxfordshire
  www.sog.org.uk/prc/oxford.html
  Parish Registers, printed, typescript, *etc.,* in the library of the Society of Genealogists

- Quaker Family History Society: Oxfordshire
  www.rootsweb.com/~engqfhs/Research/counties/oxon.htm
  Notes on Quaker records

Indexes
- IGI Batch Numbers: Oxfordshire Batch Numbers
  freepages.genealogy.rootsweb.com/~tyeroots/oxford.html

- IGI Batch Numbers for Oxford, England
  freepages.genealogy.rootsweb.com/~hughwallis/IGIBatchNumbers/CountyOxford.htm

Publications
- Oxfordshire Family History Society: Publications on Fiche & CD
  www.ofhs.org.uk/mfiche.html
  Includes parish and non-parochial registers and indexes, monumental inscriptions, *etc.*

Shropshire

Civil Registration
- Registration Districts in Shropshire
  www.fhsc.org.uk/genuki/reg/sal.htm
  Between 1837 and 1930

- Shropshire Superintendent Registrars
  www.genuki.org.uk/big/eng/SAL/SupRegistrars.html
  Addresses

Parish & Non-Parochial Registers: Introductory Pages & Lists
- Shropshire
  www.sog.org.uk/prc/shropshire.html
  Parish registers, printed, typescript, *etc.,* in the library of the Society of Genealogists

- Quaker Family History Society: Shropshire
  www.rootsweb.com/~engqfhs/Research/counties/Shrops.htm
  Notes on Quaker records

Indexes
- Shropshire Marriage Indexes
  www.genuki.org.uk/big/eng/SAL/MarriageIndexes.html
  List of offline indexes

- Burial Indexes
  www.genuki.org.uk/big/eng/SAL/BurialIndexes.html
  Details of 2 offline indexes

- IGI Batch Numbers: Shropshire Batch Numbers
  freepages.genealogy.rootsweb.com/~tyeroots/shrop.html

- IGI Batch Numbers for Shropshire, England
  freepages.genealogy.rootsweb.com/~hughwallis/IGIBatchNumbers/CountyShropshire.htm

Publications
- Shropshire Family History Society: Original Parish Registers of Shropshire available on Microfiche
  www.genuki.org.uk/big/eng/SAL/SFHS/OrigPR.html

- Miscellaneous Transcripts for Sale (photocopies)
  www.genuki.org.uk/big/eng/SAL/SFHS/Transcripts.html
  Mainly parish registers

- Shropshire Printed Parish Registers on Microfiche: Hereford Diocese
  www.genuki.org.uk/big/eng/SAL/SFHS/PR__Hereford.html

- Shropshire Printed Parish Registers on Microfiche: Lichfield Diocese
  www.genuki.org.uk/big/eng/SAL/SFHS/PR__Lichfield.html

- Shropshire Printed Parish Registers on Microfiche: St. Asaph's Diocese
  www.genuki.org.uk/big/eng/SAL/SFHS/PR__StAsaph.html

- Shropshire Printed Parish Registers on Microfiche: Nonconformist and Roman Catholic
  www.genuki.org.uk/big/eng/SAL/SFHS/Nonconformist.html

Smethcote
- The register of Smethcote
  www.uk-genealogy.org.uk/england/Shropshire/Smethcote/index.html
  Facsimile of the edition published by the Parish Register Society in 1899, covering 1609-1812

Willey
- The Register of Willey
  www.dewhirst.ndirect.co.uk/wilkfiles/willey%20registers.pdf
  Facsimile of the published edition

Somerset

Civil Registration
- Registration Districts in Somerset
  www.fhsc.org.uk/genuki/reg/som.htm
  Between 1837 and 1930

- [St. Catherine's House Marriage Index, Jan-March, 1849. District 10. Somerset/Devon]
  www.cs.ncl.ac.uk/genuki/StCathsTranscriptions/CATH4910.TXT

Parish & Non-Parochial Registers: Introductory Pages & Lists
- Parish Records
  www.somerset.gov.uk/archives/
  Click on 'Guide to Research & Holdings', and on title. List of parish registers, *etc.,* at Somerset Archives and Record Service, with pages for each parish (not otherwise listed here)

- Non-Conformist Records
  www.somerset.gov.uk/archives/NonConfRecs.htm
  General discussion of records at Somerset Record Office

- Somerset
  www.sog.org.uk/prc/som.html
  Parish registers, printed, typescript, *etc.,* in the library of the Society of Genealogists

- Location of Local Parish Registers
  www.gomezsmarts.free-online.co.uk/prs/regrlocs.htm
  From the Frome area

- Quaker Family History Society: Somerset
  www.rootsweb.com/~engqfhs/Research/counties/somerset.htm
  Notes on Quaker records

Indexes
- Somerset Genweb Births and Baptisms Index
  www.geocities.com/somersetindex/index.htm
  Compiled from submissions

- Parishes covered by Boyd's Marriage Index: Somerset
  www.englishorigins.com/bmi-parishstats.asp?county=Somerset
- Colin's Genealogy Pages: A-Z Index of Baptisms & Marriages
  genealogy.colinrayner.org.uk
  Click on title. Index to registers on this web-site (individually listed below)
- IGI Batch Numbers: Somerset Batch Numbers
  freepages.genealogy.rootsweb.com/~tyeroots/somerset.html
- IGI Batch Numbers for Somerset, England
  freepages.genealogy.rootsweb.com/~hughwallis/IGIBatchNumbers/CountySomerset.htm

Marriage Licences
- Marriage Licences
  www.somerset.gov.uk/archives/
  Click on 'Guide to Research & Holdings', and on title

Transcript Collections on the Web
See also Devon
- Baptisms, Burials and Cemetery Indexes
  home.freeuk.net/wsmfhs/bbindex.htm
  Collection of indexes to transcripts published by Weston-Super-Mare Family History Society, separately listed below
- Parish Register Transcriptions for Somerset, England
  users.bigpond.net.au/stellars/SomersetPRs/index.htm
  Collection, separately listed below
- Parish Registers
  freespace.virgin.net/paul.mansfield1/paul003.htm
  Collection of web-pages for Somerset separately listed below
- Index of Parish Transcripts
  genealogy.colinrayner.org.uk
  Click on title. Collection of Somerset parish register transcripts individually listed below
- Somerset
  freepages.genealogy.rootsweb.com/~parishregisters/somerset/somerset.htm
  Collection of parish register transcripts individually listed below

- Roy Parkhouse's Genealogy Site: Transcriptions
  www.parkhouse.org.uk/transcs/tcontent.htm
  For Somerset
- Somerset Records
  www.westcountrygenealogy.com/somerset/
  Collection of register transcriptions
- Transcriptions for Somerset
  www.genealogyhelp.co.uk/England/Somerset/Misc%20Transcriptions/Somerset%20Transcriptions.htm
  Links to transcripts of parish registers, *etc.,* mostly listed below
- Baptisms, Marriages and Burials at Anglican Churches
  www.gomezsmarts.free-online.co.uk/prs/prs.htm
  Many pages for particular parishes in the Frome area

Publications
- Publications
  home.freeuk.net/wsmfhs/publications.htm
  Of Weston-Super-Mare Family History Society, includes parish registers, monumental inscriptions, *etc.*
- Bernard D. Welshman
  www.bdwelchman.com/
  Many transcripts of Somerset and Devon parish registers for sale

Abbas Combe
- Abbas & Temple Coombe Genealogy & History: Parish & Non-Conformist Registers
  www.westcountrygenealogy.com/ses/temple_combe
  Lookups offered

Aisholt
- Aisholt Marriage Index 1654 to 1812
  www.westcountrygenealogy.com/somerset/aisholt_marriages.htm
  Actually a transcript rather than an index

Angersleigh
- Angersleigh Baptisms 1693-1901
  www.genuki.org.uk/big/eng/SOM/Angersleigh/AngBap.html

- Angersleigh Marriage Banns, 1755-1812
  www.genuki.org.uk/big/eng/SOM/Angersleigh/AngBan.html
- Angersleigh Marriages 1693-1892
  www.genuki.org.uk/big/eng/SOM/Angersleigh/AngMar.html
- Angersleigh Burials 1678-1983
  www.genuki.org.uk/big/eng/SOM/Angersleigh/AngBur.html

Ash
See Martock

Ash Priors
- Transcripts of Ash Priors Holy Trinity Parish Register: Index
  www.btinternet.com/~PBenyon/H__m__w/AshPriors/Index.html
  freepages.genealogy.rootsweb.com/~pbtyc/H__m__w/AshPriors/Index.html
  Baptisms 1700-1895; banns 1764-1782; burials 1702-1812; marriages 1701-1902

Ashbrittle
- Transcripts of "St. John the Baptist" Ashbrittle, Somerset, Bishops' transcripts 1601-1837 Index
  freepages.genealogy.rootsweb.com/~pbtyc/H__m__w/Ashb/Index.html
  www.btinternet.com/~PBenyon/H__m__w/Ashb/Index.html

Ashcott
- Ashcott Index
  genealogy.colinrayner.org.uk
  Click on 'parish transcripts index', and title. In progress

Barrington
- The Parish of Barrington
  freepages.genealogy.rootsweb.com/~parishregisters/somerset/barrington/barrington.htm
  Baptisms 1701-1894; marriages 1755-1906; burials 1813-92
- Barrington Baptisms 1781-1812
  www.genuki.org.uk/big/eng/SOM/Barrington/BapBar1781.html
  Index
- Barrington Marriages 1755-1812
  www.genuki.org.uk/big/eng/SOM/Barrington/MarBar1755.html
  Continued to 1899 on 2 further pages
- Barrington Marriage Index 1755 to 1906
  www.westcountrygenealogy.com/somerset/barrington.htm
  Transcript rather than an index
- Barrington Burials 1813-1850
  www.genuki.org.uk/big/eng/SOM/Barrington/BurBa1813.html
  Continued to 1892 at **/BurBa1851.html**

Bathealton
- [Extracted from the Burial Register for the Parish of Bathealton, Somerset 1813-1976]
  www.genuki.org.uk/big/eng/SOM/Bathealton/Burials1813-1976.txt

Batheaston
- [Extracted from the Burials Register for the Parish of Batheaston, Somerset, 1831-1846]
  www.genuki.org.uk/big/eng/SOM/Batheaston/Burials1831-1846.txt

Beckington
- Some Beckington Marriages
  www.gomezsmarts.free-online.co.uk/prs/beckmars.htm

Berkley
- Extracts from Berkley Parish Registers
  www.gomezsmarts.free-online.co.uk/prs/berklepr.htm
  Baptisms 1660-1712; marriages 1660-1754; burials 1660-1770; memorial inscriptions

Bicknoller
- [Bicknoller Baptisms 1649-69]
  freespace.virgin.net/paul.mansfield1/bickbap.txt
- [Bicknoller Baptisms 1723-1735]
  freespace.virgin.net/paul.mansfield/bickbap2.txt

Bishops Hull
- Bishops Hull Marriages 1562-1812
  www.genuki.org.uk/big/eng/SOM/BishopsHull/Bmar.html

Bishops Lydeard
- Bishops Lydeard Parish "Blessed Virgin Mary" Bishops' transcripts
  freepages.genealogy.rootsweb.com/~pbtyc/H__m__w/Bish__Lyd/lndex.html
  www.btinternet.com/~PBenyon/H__m__W/Bish__Lyd/lndex.html
  Baptisms 1700-1865; burials 1700-1865; marriages 1700-1832

Blagdon
- [Blagdon Marriages 1754-1885 & Banns 1754-1812, 1827-1885]
  users.hunterlink.net.au/~ddhms/SomersetPRs/BlagdonM.csv

Bower Hinton
See Martock

Brewham
- Brewham Marriage Index 1761 to 1837
  www.westcountrygenealogy.com/somerset/brewham.htm
  Transcript rather than index

Bridgwater
- [Bridgwater Baptisms 1661-1714]
  freespace.virgin.net/paul.mansfield1/bridbap.txt
  Continued to 1743 on 3 further pages. See also index page at
  /bribainx.txt

- [Bridgwater Baptisms 1728-1743]
  freespace.virgin.net/paul.mansfield1/brid730.txt

- Bridgwater Marriages 1661-1700
  freespace.virgin.net/paul.mansfield1/bridmarr.txt
  See also index at **/bridminx.txt**

- Bridgwater Burials 1661-1714
  freespace.virgin.net/paul__mansfield1/bridbur.txt
  See also index at **/bribuinx.txt**

- Names Extracted from the Burial Register for the Parish of Bridgwater St. Mary, Somerset, 1827-1833
  www.genuki.org.uk/big/eng/SOM/Bridgwater/MaryBurials1827-1833.txt

Brompton Regis
- Transcripts of Brompton Regis "The Blessed Virgin Mary" Parish Registers
  freepages.genealogy.rootsweb.com/~pbtyc/H__m__w/ Brompton__Regis/lndex.html
  Baptisms 1751-1882; burials 1751-1870; marriages 1754-1900

- Names Extracted from the Burial Register for the parish of Brompton Regis, Somerset, 1813-1864
  www.genuki.org.uk/big/eng/SOM/BromptonRegis/Burials1813-1864.txt

Broomfield
- [Broomfield Baptisms 1701-1800]
  freespace.virgin.net/paul.mansfield1/broombap.txt
  Continued to 1845 at **/broombl3.txt**
  See also index page **/broobinx.txt**

- Broomfield Marriages
  www.westcountrygenealogy.com/somerset/broomfield__marriages.htm

Brushford
- Names Extracted from the Burials Register for the Parish of Brushford, Somerset 1813-1905
  www.genuki.org.uk/big/eng/SOM/Brushford/Burials1813-1905.txt

Bruton
- Bruton Parish Records
  freepages.genealogy.rootsweb.com/~parishregisters/somerset/bruton/ bruton.htm
  Marriages 1681-1812; Baptisms and burials forthcoming

Burrington
- [Burrington Burials 1878-1889]
  users.hunterlink.net.au/~ddhms/SomersetPRs/BurringtonB.csv

Burtle
- Burtle Transcript Index
  genealogy.colinrayner.org.uk
  Click on 'parish transcript index' and name. Baptisms 1840-59.
  In progress

47

Cannington
- Cannington Baptisms 1714-1770
  freespace.virgin.net/paul.mansfield1/cannbap.txt
  See also index page **/cann.binx.txt**
- [Cannington Marriages, 1713-1754]
  freespace.virgin.net/paul.mansfield1/cannmar.txt
  See also index page at **/cann.minx.txt**
- Names Extracted from the Burial Register for the Parish of Cannington, Somerset, 1813-1848
  www.genuki.org.uk/big/eng/SOM/Cannington/Burials1813-1848.txt

Carhampton
- Baptisms in the Parish of Carhampton, Somerset, 1763-1773
  www.genuki.org.uk/big/eng/SOM/Carhampton/BapCar__1763.html
  Continued to 1858 on 4 further pages
- Carhampton, Somerset: Banns of Marriage 1824-1882
  www.genuki.org.uk/big/eng/SOM/Carhampton/1824-1882.bann.txt
- Marriages in the Parish of Carhampton, Somerset, 1754-1767
  www.genuki.org.uk/big/eng/SOM/Carhampton/MarCar1754.html
  Continued to 1836 on 3 further pages

Catcott
- Catcott Transcript Index
  genealogy.colinrayner.org.uk
  Click on 'parish transcript index' and name. Baptisms 1820-29. In progress.

Charlton Mackrell
- Transcript from Charlton Mackrell Parish Registers: Marriages 1813-1837
  freepages.genealogy.rootsweb.com/~pbtyc/H__m__w/Charlton__Mackrell/Charlton__M__Mar__1813__37.html

Charlynch
- Charlynch Marriages
  www.westcountrygenealogy.com/somerset/charlynch__marriages.htm

Chilton Trinity
- [Chilton Trinity Baptisms 1733-1746]
  freespace.virgin.net/paul.mansfield1/chiltbap.txt
- [Chilton Trinity Marriages 1733-1746]
  freespace.virgin.net/paul.mansfield1/chiltmarr.txt
- [Chilton Trinity Burials 1732-1746]
  freespace.virgin.net/paul.mansfield1/chiltbur.txt

Chilton Polden
- Chilton Polden Transcript Index
  genealogy.colinrayner.org.uk
  Click on 'parish transcript index' and name. In progress.

Chipstable
- Transcription from All Saints Parish Registers, Chipstable, Somerset from the E. Dwelly Transcriptions
  freepages.genealogy.rootsweb.com/~pbtyc/H__m__w/Chipstable/Index.html
  www.btinternet.com/~PBenyon/H__m__w/Chipstable/Index.html
  Index to selected entries only

Clevedon
- Clevedon Civic Society: Parish & Census Records
  www.clevedon-civic-society.org.uk/weddings/Firstpage.htm
  Includes transcript of marriages 1600-1923, also indexes of baptisms and burials

Compton Pauncefoot
- Transcript of the Bishops' transcripts of the "Blessed Virgin Mary" Church of England at Compton Pauncefoot, Somerset: Baptisms 1602-1663
  freepages.genealogy.rootsweb.com/~pbtyc/H__m__w/Compton__P/Baps/Bap__1602-1663__1.html
  www.btinternet.com/~PBenyon/H__m__w/Compton__P/Index.html
  Continued to 1851 on 5 further pages
- Transcript of the Bishops' transcripts of the Blessed Virgin Mary Church of England at Compton Pauncefoot, Somerset: Marriages 1603-1663
  freepages.genealogy.rootsweb.com/~pbtyc/H__m__w/Compton__P/Mar/Mar__1603-1663__1.html
  Continued to 1841 on 3 further pages

- Transcript of the Bishops' transcripts of the Blessed Virgin Mary Church of England at Compton Pauncefoot, Somerset: Burials 1602-1663
  freepages.genealogy.rootsweb.com/~pbtyc/H__m__w/Compton__P/Bur/Bur__1602-1663__1.html
  Continued to 1851 on 2 further pages

Congresbury
- Congresbury, Somerest, England; Marriages & Banns 1754-1790; Marriages 1790-1812
  users.bigpond.net.au/stellers/SomersetPRs/CongresburyM.txt

Corfe
- Corfe St. Nicholas Baptisms 1682-1894
  www.genuki.org.uk/big/eng/SOM/Corfe/BapCor.html
  Index

- Corfe Marriage Banns 1779-1824
  www.genuki.org.uk/big/eng/SOM/Corfe/BanCor1.html
  Continued to 1936 at **/BanCor2.html**

- Corfe Marriages 1776-1878
  www.genuki.org.uk/big/eng/SOM/Corfe/MarCor.html

- Corfe, St. Nicholas Burials 1678-1899
  www.genuki.org.uk/big/eng/SOM/Corfe/BurCor.html
  Index

Curry Rivel
- Curry Rivel Marriage Index 1642 to 1812
  www.westcountrygenealogy.com/somerset/curry__rivel.htm
  Transcript, not an index

Ditcheat
- Parish Registers of Ditcheat, Somerset
  www.math.mun.ca/~dapike/family-history/ditcheat.htm
  Extracts, 1562-1891

Dodington
- Dodington Marriages 1540 to 1805
  www.westcountrygenealogy.com/somerset/dodington__marriages.htm

Drayton
- Drayton Marriage Index 1558 to 1812
  www.westcountrygenealogy.com/somerset/drayton.htm
  Transcript, rather than index

Dunster
- Baptisms in the Parish of St. George, Dunster, 1716-1721
  www.genuki.org.uk/big/eng/SOM/BapDun__1716.html
  Continued to 1903 on 25 further pages

- Dunster, Somerset: Banns of Marriage 1754-1812
  www.genuki.org.uk/big/eng/SOM/Dunster/17541812.banns.txt

- Dunster, St. George, Somerset. Marriages 1717-1757
  www.genuki.org.uk/big/eng/SOM/Dunster/17171757.mar.txt
  Continued as follows:
  1813-1836 **/18131836.mar.txt**
  1837-1901 **/18371901.mar.txt**

Durleigh
- [Durleigh Baptisms 1737-1880]
  freespace.virgin.net/paul.mansfield1/durlbap.txt

- Durleigh Marriages 1683 to 1807
  www.westcountrygenealogy.com/somerset/durleigh__marriages.htm

- [Durleigh Burials 1760-1870
  freespace.virgin.net/paul.mansfield1/durlbur.txt

Durston
- [Durston Baptisms 1712-1812
  freespace.virgin.net/paul.mansfield1/durstbap.txt

East Coker
- East Coker Burials 1813-1885
  www.genuki.org.uk/big/eng/SOM/EastCoker/BurEC.html
  Index

Edington
- Edington Transcript Index
  www.colinrayner.org.uk
  Click on 'parish transcript index' and name. Baptisms 1810-60. In progress.

Enmore

- [Enmore Baptisms 1653-1886]
  freespace.virgin.net/paul.mansfield1/enmorbap.txt
  See also index page at **/enmbainx.txt**

- [Enmore Marriages 1653-1703]
  freespace.virgin.net/paul.mansfield1/enmormar.txt

- [Enmore Marriages 1655 to 1811]
  www.westcountrygenealogy.com/somerset/enmore_marriages.htm

- [Enmore Burials 1653-1812]
  freespace.virgin.net/paul.mansfield1/enmorbur.txt

Fitzhead

- Extracts from Fitzhead Parish registers: Baptisms
  freepages.genealogy.rootsweb.com/~pbtyc/H__m__w/Fitzhead/Fitz-Bap__A-F__1.html
  Index, continued on 2 further pages

- Extracts from Fitzhead Parish Registers: Marriages
  freepages.genealogy.rootsweb.com/~pbtyc/H__m__w/Fitzhead/Fitz__Mar__A-K__1.html
  Index, continued at **/Fitz__Mar__L-Z__1.html**

- Extracts from Fitzhead Parish Registers: Burials
  freepages.genealogy.rootsweb.com/~pbtyc/H__m__w/Fitzhead/Fitz__Bur.1.html
  Index

Fivehead

- The Parish of Fivehead
  freepages.genealogy.rootsweb.com/~parishregisters/somerset/fivehead/fivehead.htm
  Baptisms 1802-1898; Marriages 1813-1845; Burials 1803-1887

Frome

- Frome Nonconformist Records in the Public Record Office
  www.gomezsmarts.free-online.co.uk/prs/rg4frome.htm

- Burials at the Quaker Burials Ground in Frome
  www.gomezsmarts.co.uk/prs/quakburs.htm

- Miscellaneous Marriages in Frome and its Hundred
  www.gomezsmarts.free-online.co.uk/prs/spouses.html
  Submitted extracts

Glastonbury

- Glastonbury St. Benedict Transcript Index
  www.colinrayner.org.uk
  Click on 'Parish transcripts index' and name. Baptisms 1800-1849; marriages 1800-1839. In progress.

- Glastonbury St. John Transcript Index
  genealogy.colinrayner.org.uk
  Click on 'parish transcript index' and name. Marriages 1810-14. In progress.

Goathurst

- [Goathurst Baptisms 1749-1812]
  freespace.virgin.net/paul.mansfield1/goath17.txt

- [Goathurst Baptisms 1813-1870]
  freespace.virgin.net/paul.mansfield1/goathbap.txt
  See also index at **/goatbaix.txt**

Godney

- Godney Transcript Index
  genealogy.colinrayner.org.uk
  Click on 'Parish Transcript index' and name. Baptisms 1840-49. In progress.

Halse

- Transcript of Halse Parish Registers
  freepages.genealogy.rootsweb.com/~Pbenyon/H__m__w/Halse/Index.html
  Includes baptisms, banns, marriages and burials

- Halse Marriages 1559-1812
  www.genuki.org.uk/big/eng/SOM/Halse/Hmar.html
  Index

Henstridge

- Hestridge Genealogy & History: Parish & Non-conformist registers
  www.westcountrygenealogy.com/ses/henstridge/
  Marriages, 1605 to 1754

Holton
- Holton Genealogy & History: Parish & Non-Conformist Registers
  www.westcountrygenealogy.com/ses/holton/
  Marriages, 1558-1704

Horsington
- Horsington Genealogy & History: Parish & Non-Conformist Registers
  www.westcountrygenealogy.com/ses/horsington/
  Marriages, 1559-1754

Huish Champflower
- Transcript of Huish Champflower St. Peter's Parish Registers
  freepages.genealogy.rootsweb.com/~pbtyc/H_m_w/Huish_Champ/Index.html
  Baptisms 1786-1873; burials 1807-1902; marriages 1755-1900

Hutton
- Hutton Baptism Records
  home.freeuk.net/wsmfhs/hutbaptism.htm
  Index, 1813-37, to a published transcript
- Hutton, Somerset, England: Marriages 1754-1812, 1813-1837; Banns 1825-1901
  users.bigpond.net.au/~stellars/SomersetPRs/HuttonM.txt
- Hutton Burial Records
  home.freeuk.net/wsmfhs/hutburials.htm
  Index, 1813-37, to a published transcript

Isle Abbots
- The Parish of Isle Abbotts
  freepages.genealogy.rootsweb.com/~parishregisters/somerset/isleabbotts/isleabbotts.htm
  Baptisms 1813-1900; marriages 1754-1900; burials 1813-1946
- Isle Abotts Marriage Index, 1755 to 1900
  www.westcountrygenealogy.com/somerset/isle_abbotts.htm
  Transcript, rather than index

Kewstoke
- Names Extracted from the Burial Register for the parish of Kewstoke, Somerset, 1813-1855
  www.genuki.org.uk/big/eng/SOM/Kewstoke/Burials1813-1855.txt

Kingsbury Episcopi
- The Parish of Kingsbury Episcopi
  freepages.genealogy.rootsweb.com/~parishregisters/somerset/Kingsbury/Kingsbury.htm
  Baptisms 1813-1855; Marriages 1837-1879
- Kingsbury Episcopi Marriages 1813-1837
  www.genuki.org.uk/big/eng/SOM/KingsburyEpiscopi/MarKE1813.html
  Continued to 1863 on 2 further pages

Kingston
- Kingston St. Mary Baptisms 1772-1812
  www.genuki.org.uk/big/eng/SOM/Kingston/BapKin.html
  Index
- Kingston St. Mary Burials 1763-1812
  www.genuki.org.uk/big/eng/SOM/Kingston/BurKin.hmtl
  Index

Kittisford
- Transcription from "All Saints" Parish Registers, Kittisford, Somerset from E. Dwelly Transcriptions 1694-1836: Index
  freepages.genealogy.rootsweb.com/~pbtyc/H_m_w/Kittisford/Index.html
  www.btinternet.com/~PBenyon/H_m_w/Kittisford/Index.html
- Index to Transcription from All Saints Parish Register, Kittisford, Somerset: Marriages. From E. Dwelly transcriptions 1694-1836
  freepages.genealogy.rootsweb.com/~pbtyc/H_m_w/Kittisford/Mar/Index.html
- Transcription of All Saints Parish Registers, Kittisford, Somerset: Burials. From E. Dwelly Transcriptions 1694-1836
  freepages.genealogy.rootsweb.com/~pbtyc/H_m_w/Kittisford/Bur/Index.html
  Index

Leigh upon Mendip
- Leigh upon Mendip Marriages 1754-1837
  www.gomezsmarts.co.uk/prs/leigmars.htm

Locking
- Locking Birth / Baptism Records 1750-1812
  home.freeuk.net/wsmfhs/lockbaptism1750.htm
  Continued to 1837 at /lockbaptism.htm
  Indexes to a published transcript

- Locking Marriage Records 1755-1808
  home.freeuk.net/wsmfhs/lockmar1755-1808.htm
  Continued to 1836 at /lockmar1813-1836
  Indexes to a published transcript

- Locking Burial Records 1778-1812
  home.freeuk.net/wsmfhs/lockburial.htm
  Index to a published transcript

Long Load
- Long Load Marriage Index 1749 to 1808
  www.westcountrygenealogy.com/somerset/long__load.htm
  Transcript rather than index
  See also Martock

Loxton
- Parish Records
  www.loxtonsomerset.org.uk/records.html
  Loxton baptisms 1800-1900, marriages 1754-1900 and burials 1776-1920. In progress.

Lullington
- Extracts from Lullington Parish Registers
  www.gomezsmarts.free-online.co.uk/prs/lullingt.htm
  Baptisms 1725-1805 & 1808-12; marriages 1713-1837; burials 1712-1807 & 1812

Maperton
- Maperton Genealogy & History Parish and Non-Conformist Registers
  www.westcountrygenealogy.com/ses/maperton/
  Includes marriages, 1556-1754

Marston Bigot
- Extracts from Marston Bigot Parish Registers
  www.gomezsmarts.free-online.co.uk/prs/marstonb.htm
  Selected marriages, 1657-1890, with memorial inscriptions

Marston Magna
- Marston Magna Marriages 1562 to 1753
  www.westcountrygenealogy.com/somerset/marston__magna__marriages.htm

Martock
- Parish Records: Martock
  www.genealogyhelp.co.uk/Martock%20Web%20Site/parish%20records.htm
  Martock baptisms 1700-1889; burials 1660-1901; marriages 1559-1812. Also includes Ash baptisms 1845-94; marriages 1846-1975; burials 1845-1964; Bower Hinton Chapel baptisms 1788-1826; marriages 1837-1998; burials 1834-1951; funerals 1951-97; *etc.* Registers for Long Load forthcoming

- Martock Marriage Index 1661 to 1760
  www.westcountrygenealogy.com/somerset/martock__1661to1760.htm
  Transcript, rather than index

- Martock Marriage Index 1761 to 1812
  www.westcountrygenealogy.com/somerset/martock__1761to1812.htm
  Transcript, rather than index

Meare
- Meare Transcript Index
  genealogy.colinrayner.org.uk
  Click on 'Parish Transcript Index' and name. Baptisms 1790-1859; marriages 1790-1859; burials 1813-29. In progress

Mells
- Extracts from Mells Parish Registers
  www.gomezsmarts.free-online.co.uk/prs/mellsbmd.htm

Milborne Port
- Milborne Port Genealogy & History: Parish & Non-Conformist Registers
  www.westcountrygenealogy.com/ses/milborne__port
  Click on 'parish registers'. Includes marriage index, 1538-1799

Milverton
- Extracts from Parish Registers from Milverton, Somerset: Baptisms
  freepages.genealogy.rootsweb.com/~pbtyc/H_m_w/Mil/Baps/A-Betty.html
  Alphabetical. Continued on 9 further pages
- Extracts from Parish Registers from Milverton, Somerset: Banns
  freepages.genealogy.rootsweb.com/~pbtyc/H_m_w/Mil/Ban/A-E.html
  Alphabetical. Continued on 2 further pages
- Extracts from Parish Registers from Milverton, Somerset: Marriages
  freepages.genealogy.rootsweb.com/~pbtyc/H_m_w/Mil/Mar/A-B.html
  Alphabetical. Continued on 8 further pages
- Extracts from Parish Registers from Milverton, Somerset: Burials
  freepages.genealogy.rootsweb.com/~pbtyc/H_m_w/Mil/Bur/A-B.html
  Alphabetical. Continued on 10 further pages.
- Extracts from Milverton, Somerset Independent Birth & Baptism Register 1783-1837
  freepages.genealogy.rootsweb.com/~pbtyc/H_m_w/Milv_Ind/Mil_Ind.htm
  www.btinternet.com/~PBenyon/H_m_w/Milv_Ind/Mil_Ind.html

Minehead
- Baptisms in the Parish of Minehead, Somerset: 1715-1719
  www.genuki.org.uk/big/eng/SOM/Minehead/BapMin_1715.html
  Continued to 1901 on 27 further pages
- Minehead Marriages 1776-1815
  www.genuki.org.uk/big/eng/SOM/Minehead/MarMi1776.html
  Continued to 1900 on 4 further pages
- Minehead Burials 1807-1812
  www.genuki.org.uk/big/eng/SOM/Minehead/BurMi1807.html
  Continued to 1901 on 4 further pages
- Quaker Burials at Minehead, 1701-1705
  www.genuki.org.uk/big/eng/SOM/Minehead/QuakerBurials1701.html

Nether Stowey
- [Nether Stowey Baptism 1671-1700]
  freespace.virgin.net/paul.mansfield1/netst671.txt
- [Nether Stowey Marriages 1671-1700]
  freespace.virgin.net/paul.mansfield1/netstm71.txt
- [Nether Stowey Burials 1671-1700]
  freespace.virgin.net/paul.mansfield1/netstb71.txt

North Barrow
- North Barrow Marriages 1568 to 1694
  www.westcountrygenealogy.com/somerset/north_barrow_marriages.htm
  Transcript, rather than index

North Cheriton
- North Cheriton Genealogy & History: Parish and Non-Conformist Registers
  www.westcountrygenealogy.com/ses/north_cheriton/
  Click on 'parish registers'. Marriages 1600-1744

Norton Fitzwarren
- Norton Fitzwarren, Somerset: Baptisms 1726-1812
  homepages.rootsweb.com/~mwi/somnfwc1.txt
- Norton Fitzwarren, Somerset: Marriages 1726-1791
  homepages.rootsweb.com/~mwi/somnfwm1.txt
- Norton Fitzwarren Marriages 1726-1791
  www.genuki.org.uk/big/eng/SOM/Norton Fitzwarren/MarNor.html
  Index
- Norton Fitzwarren Burials 1726-1780
  www.genuki.org.uk/big/eng/SOM/NortonFitzwarren/BurNor.html
  Index

Nunney
- Extracts from Nunney Parish Registers
  www.gomezsmarts.free-online.co.uk/prs/nunneypr.htm
  Baptisms 1685-1750; marriages 1700-1904; burials 1718-49; monumental inscriptions. See also **/nunneymix.htm** for marriage index

Nynehead
- Nynehead, Somerset: Baptisms 1769-1812
  homepages.rootsweb.com/~mwi/somnync1.txt

- Nynehead Baptisms 1769-1812
  www.genuki.org.uk/big/eng/SOM/Nynehead/BapNyn.html
  Index

- Nynehead Burials 1769-1812
  www.genuki.org.uk/big/eng/SOM/Nynehead/BurNyn.html
  Index

Oake
- Oake Baptisms 1793-1812
  www.genuki.org.uk/big/eng/SOM/Oake/BapOak.html

- Oake Burials 1793-1812
  www.genuki.org.uk/big/eng/SOM/Oake/BurOak.html
  Index

Otterford
- Otterford Baptisms 1567-1900
  www.genuki.org.uk/big/eng/SOM/Otterford/OttBap.html
  Index

- Otterford Marriages 1585-1900
  www.genuki.org.uk/big/eng/SOM/Otterford/OttMar.html

- Otterford Burials 1558-1903
  www.genuki.org.uk/big/eng/SOM/Otterford/OttBur.html
  Index

Otterhampton
- Otterhampton Marriages 1656 to 1771
  www.westcountrygenealogy.com/somerset/otterhampton_marriages.htm

Over Stowey
- Overstowey Marriages 1558 to 1811
  www.westcountrygenealogy.com/somerset/overstowey_marriages.htm

Pitminster
- Pitminster, St. Mary and St. Andrew: Baptisms 1649-1885
  www.genuki.org.uk/big/eng/SOM/Pitminster/BapPit.html
  Index

- Pitminster, St. Mary and St. Andrew, Somerset: Baptisms 1813-1885
  homepages.rootsweb.com/~mwi/sompit18.txt

- Pitminster, St. Mary and St. Andrew: Marriage Banns 1754-1810
  www.genuki.org.uk/big/eng/SOM/Pitminster/PitBann.html
  Index

- Pitminster Marriages 1673-1885
  www.genuki.org.uk/big/eng/SOM/Pitminster/MarPit.html
  Index

- Pitminster, St. Mary and St. Andrew: Burials 1683-1886
  www.genuki.org.uk/big/eng/SOM/Pitminster/BurPit.html
  Index

Pitney
- The Parish of Pitney
  freepages.genealogy.rootsweb.com/~parishregisters/somerset/pitney/pitney.htm
  Baptisms 1734-1880; marriages 1735-1900; burials 1735-1812

- Pitney Baptisms 1734-1812
  www.genuki.org.uk/big/eng/SOM/Pitney/BapPi1734.html
  Continued to 1870 on 2 further pages

- Pitney Marriages 1735-1859
  www.genuki.org.uk/big/eng/SOM/Pitney/MarPit1735.html
  Continued to 1899 at **/MarPit1860.html**

- Pitney Burials 1734-1812
  www.genuki.org.uk/big/eng/SOM/Pitney/BurPi1735.html

Priston
- Baptisms and Burials for 1871 in Priston, Somerset
  www.genuki.org.uk/big/eng/SOM/Priston/BapsBurs1871.txt

Puckington
- Puckington Marriages 1813-1834
  freepages.genealogy.rootsweb.com/~parishregisters/somerset/puckington/puckington_Marriages_1813-1834.htm

Pylle
- Pylle Marriages 1591 to 1799
  www.westcountrygenealogy.com/somerset/pyle__marriages.htm

Queen Camel
- Queen Camel Marriages 1601 to 1753
  www.westcountrygenealogy.com/somerset/queen__camel__marriages.htm

Raddington
- Transcriptions from St. Michael's Parish Register, Raddington, Somerest. From E. Dwelly transcriptions for the period 1814-1836
  freepages.genealogy.rootsweb.com/~pbtyc/H__m__w/Raddington/Baps/Bap.html

Roddon
- Extracts from Roddon Parish Registers
  www.gomezsmarts.free-online.co.uk/prs/roddenpr.htm
  Baptisms 1767-1840; marriages 1754-1837; burials 1765-1812

Rode
- Headstone Information from Rode Baptist Chapel Burial Ground
  www.gomezsmarts.free-online.co.uk/prs/rodebcmi.htm

St. Michael Church
- [St. Michael Church Baptisms 1695-1802]
  freespace.virgin.net/paul.mansfield1/stmicbap.txt

Sampford Brett
- [Sampford Brett Baptisms 1691-1737]
  freespace.virgin.net/paul.mansfield1/sampbap.txt
- [Sampford Brett Marriages 1692-1737]
  freespace.virgin.net/paul.mansfield1/sampmar.txt
- [Sampford Brett Burials 1654-1676 & 1692-1737]
  freespace.virgin.net/paul.mansfield1/sampbur.txt
  See also index **/sampbind.txt**

Shapwick
- Shapwick Transcript Index
  genealogy.colinrayner.org.uk
  Click on 'Parish Transcript Index' and name. Baptisms 1840-59. In progress

Shepton Beauchamp
- The Parish of Shepton Beauchamp
  freepages.genealogy.rootsweb.com/~parishregisters/somerset/shepton/shepton.htm
  Baptisms 1845-1900; marriages 1837-1900

Shipham
- Shipham Banns 1756-1812; marriages 1756-1812; marriages 1813-1837
  users.bigpond.net.au/~stellars/SomersetPRs/ShiphamM.csv

South Barrow
- South Barrow Marriages 1580 to 1753
  www.westcountrygenealogy.com/somerset/south__barrow__marriages.htm

Spaxton
- Spaxton Baptisms 1688-1734
  www.genuki.org.uk/big/eng/SOM/Spaxton/BapSpa.html
  Index
- Spaxton Burials 1688-1729
  www.genuki.org.uk/big/eng/SOM/Spaxton/BurSpa.html
  Index

Stanton Prior
- Baptisms, 1839-1858, Stanton Prior, Somerset
  www.genuki.org.uk/big/eng/SOM/StantonPrior/Baptisms1839-1858.txt
  From bishops' transcripts
- Burials 1839-1860, Stanton Prior, Somerset
  www.genuki.org.uk/big/eng/SOM/StantonPrior/Burials1839-1860.html
  From bishops' transcripts

Stockland Gaunt
- Stockland Gaunts Marriages 1538 to 1760
  www.westcountrygenealogy.com/somerset/
  Click on title.

Stocklinch Ottersey
- Stocklinch Ottersey Baptisms 1558-1660
  www.genuki.org.uk/big/eng/SOM/StocklinchOttersey/BapStL.html

Stogumber

- [Stogumber Baptisms 1658-1682]
  freespace.virgin.net/paul.mansfield1/stogbap.txt
  See also index at **/stogbinx.txt**

- [Stogumber Marriages 1658-1712]
  freespace.virgin.net/paul.mansfield1/stogmarr.txt
  See also index at **/stogmind.txt**

- [Stogumber Burials 1658-1685]
  freespace.virgin.net/paul.mansfield1/stogbur.txt
  See also index **/stogbuix.txt**

Stoke St. Mary

- Stoke St. Mary Magdalene Baptisms 1677-1812
  www.genuki.org.uk/big/eng/SOM/StokeStMary/BapSto.html
  Index

- Stoke St. Mary Magdalene Marriages 1723-1748
  www.genuki.org.uk/big/eng/SOM/StokeStMary/MarSto.html
  Index

- Stoke St. Mary Magdalene Burials 1679-1812
  www.genuki.org.uk/big/eng/SOM/StokeStMary/BurSto.html
  Index

Stoke sub Hamdon

- Stoke sub Hamdon Baptisms 1720-1812
  www.genuki.org.uk/big/eng/SOM/StokeSubHamdon/BapStH.html

- Stoke Sub Hamdon Burials 1721-1812
  www.genuki.org.uk/big/eng/SOM/StokeSubHamdon/BurStH.html
  Index

Stoke Trister

- Marriages at Stoke Trister 1752-1812
  www.westcountrygenealogy.com/ses/marriages.htm

Stowell

- Stowell Marriages 1654 to 1836
  www.westcountrygenealogy.com/ses/stowell__marriages.htm

Stratton on the Fosse

- Baptisms 1599 to 1812 at Stratton-on-the-Fosse, Somerset
  www.genuki.org.uk/big/eng/SOM/StrattonOnTheFosse/
  Baptisms1599-1812.txt

- Baptisms 1813-1837 at Stratton-on-the-Fosse, Somerset, England
  www.genuki.org.uk/big/eng/SOM/StrattonOnTheFosse/
  Baptisms1813-1837.txt
  From bishops' transcripts

- Banns 1755 to 1788 at Stratton-on-the-Fosse, Somerset
  www.genuki.org.uk/big/eng/SOM/StrattonOnTheFosse/
  Banns1755-1788.txt

- Marriages 1599 to 1812 at Stratton-on-the-Fosse, Somerset
  www.genuki.org.uk/big/eng/SOM/StrattonOnTheFosse/
  Marriages1599-1812.txt

- Marriages 1813-1837 at Stratton-on-the-Fosse, Somerset
  www.genuki.org.uk/big/eng/SOM/StrattonOnTheFosse/
  Marriages1813-1837.txt
  From bishops' transcripts

- Burials 1599 to 1812 at Stratton-on-the-Fosse, Somerset
  www.genuki.org.uk/big/eng/SOM/StrattonOnTheFosse/
  Burials1599-1812.txt

- Burials 1813-1837 at Stratton-on-the-Fosse, Somerset
  www.genuki.org.uk/big/eng/SOM/StrattonOnTheFosse/
  Burials1813-1837.txt

Sutton Montis

- Sutton Montis (Montague) Marriages 1603 to 1754
  www.westcountrygenealogy.com/somerset/
  sutton__montis__marriages.htm

Swell

- The Parish of Swell
  freepages.genealogy.rootsweb.com/~parishregisters/somerset/swell/
  swell.htm>

  Baptisms 1813-1981; marriages 1754-1974; burials 1813-1982

Taunton

- Taunton St. James Baptisms 1610-1620
  www.genuki.org.uk/big/eng/SOM/Taunton/BapTs1.html
  Index

- Taunton St. James Baptisms 1683-1694
  www.genuki.org.uk/big/eng/SOM/Taunton/BapTs2.html
  Index

- [Baptisms at Taunton (St. James) 1696-1718]
  freespace.virgin.net/paul.mansfield1/taunjbap.txt
  See also index at **/taunjbix.txt**

- Taunton, St. James, Marriages 1610-1620
  www.genuki.org.uk/big/eng/SOM/Taunton/MarsTsj.html
  Index

- Taunton St. James Burials 1610-1620
  www.genuki.org.uk/big/eng/SOM/Taunton/BurTsj.html
  Index

- [Taunton: Mary Magdalene Baptisms 1685-1695]
  freespace.virgin.net/paul.mansfield1/taunmbap.txt
  See also index at **/taumbaix.txt**

- Taunton Mary Magdalene 1708-1717
  freespace.virgin.net/paul.mansfield1/taunm708.txt
  Baptisms. Continued as follows:
  1718-27 **/taunmba3.txt**
  1728-34 **/taunm728.txt**
  1735-50 **/taunmba4.txt**
  1751-67 **/taunmba2.txt**

- Taunton St. Mary's Marriages 1728-1812
  www.genuki.org.uk/big/eng/SOM/Taunton/Tmar.html
  Index

Templecombe
See Abbas Combe

Thurlbear

- Thurlbear Baptisms 1700-1901
  www.genuki.org.uk/big/eng/SOM/Thurlbear/BapThu.html
  Index

- Thurlbear Marriages 1700-1900
  www.genuki.org.uk/big/eng/SOM/Thurlbear/MarThu.html
  Index

- Thurlbear, St. Thomas Burials 1700-1810
  www.genuki.org.uk/big/eng/SOM/Thurlbear/BurThu.html
  Index

Thurloxton

- Thurloxton Baptisms 1559-1696
  www.genuki.org.uk/big/eng/SOM/Thurloxton/BapThu.html

- Thurloxton Marriages 1559-1689
  www.genuki.org.uk/big/eng/SOM/Thurloxton/MarThu.html
  Index

- Thurloxton Burials 1559-1693
  www.genuki.org.uk/big/eng/SOM/Thurloxton/BurThu.html
  Index

Trull

- Trull, All Saints Baptisms 1669-1925
  www.genuki.org.uk/big/eng/SOM/Trull/BapTru.html
  Index

- Trull Marriage Banns 1755-1817
  www.genuki.org.uk/big/eng/SOM/Trull/TruBan.html
  Index

- Trull Marriages 1677-1944
  www.genuki.org.uk/big/eng/SOM/Trull/MarTru.html
  Index

- Trull, All Saints, Somerset: Burials 1678-1889
  homepages.rootsweb.com/~mwi/allsaint.txt

- Trull All Saints Burials 1678-1889
  www.genuki.org.uk/big/eng/SOM/Trull/Burtru.html
  Index

Uphill
- Uphill Baptism Records
  home.freeuk.net/wsmfhs/upbaptism.htm
  Index, 1813-37, to a published transcript
- Uphill Burial Records
  home.freeuk.net/wsmfhs/upburial.htm
  Index, 1813-37, to a published transcript

Wedmore
- Wedmore Genealogy Pages
  www.tutton.org/parrec.html
  Includes indexes to baptisms 1561-1812 and marriages 1561-1839.
  In progress

Wellington
- Wellington St. John, Somerset
  www.genuki.org.uk/big/eng/SOM/Wellington/Transcripts/
  Baptisms 1683-1812; marriages 1683-1783; burials 1683-1812
- Transcripts: Wellington Independent Births and Baptisms
  freepages.genealogy.rootsweb.com/~pbtyc/H__m__w/well/
  Well__Ind__Bir__A-B__1.html
  Alphabetical. Continued on 6 further pages
- Transcripts: Wellington Independent Births and Burials
  freepages.genealogy.rootsweb.com/~pbtyc/H__m__w/Well/
  Well__Ind__Bur__A-F__1.html
  Alphabetical. Continued on 2 further pages

West Buckland
- West Buckland Baptisms 1702-1886
  www.genuki.gov.uk/big/eng/SOM/WestBuckland/WBBap.html
  Index
- West Buckland Marriages 1702-1885
  www.genuki.org.uk/big/eng/SOM/WestBuckland/WBMar.html
- West Buckland Burials 1702-1885
  www.genuki.org.uk/big/eng/SOM/WestBuckland/WBBur.html
  Index

West Hatch
- West Hatch Marriage Index 1604 to 1782
  www.westcountrygenealogy.com/somerset/west__hatch__marriages.htm

Weston Bampfylde
- Weston Bamflyde Marriages 1591 to 1754
  www.westcountrygenealogy.com/somerset/weston__bamflyde__marriages.htm

Weston super Mare
- Weston Super Mare Baptism Records
  home.freeuk.net/wsmfhs/westonbaptism.htm
  Index, 1813-37, to a published transcript
- Weston Super Mare Burial Records
  home.freeuk.net.wsmfhs/westonburial.htm
  Index, 1813-37, to a published transcript

Wincanton
- Parish and Non-Conformist Registers: Wincanton (St. Peter and St. Paul)
  www.westcountrygenealogy.com/ses/wincanton/parishregisters.htm
  Baptisms 1721-31; marriages 1607-1757; burials 1721-40.

Winscombe
- St. James the Great, Winscombe: Christenings, 1737-1799
  www.pencoed-wales.freeserve.co.uk/winscombe__baptisms1.htm
- St. James the Great, Winscombe: Banns of Marriage 1754-1811
  www.pencoed-wales.freeserve.co.uk/winscombe__banns1.html
- St. James the Great, Winscombe: Marriages 1737-1754
  www.pencoed-wales.freeserve.co.uk/winscombe__marriages1.htm
  Continued to 1800 at /winscombe__marriages2.htm
- St. James the Great, Winscombe; Burials 1736-1799
  www.pencoed-wales.freeserve.co.uk/winscombe__burials1.htm

Witham Friary
- Extracts from Witham Friary Parish Registers
  www.gomezsmarts.free-online.co.uk/prs/withamf.htm
  Baptisms 1695-1900; banns, 1823-77; marriages 1695-1900; burials 1813-1900.

Withycombe
- Baptisms in the Parish of St. Nicholas, Withycombe, Somerset, 1683-1700
  www.genuki.org.uk/big/eng/SOM/Withycombe/BapWit1683
  Continued to 1897 on 6 further pages

- Marriages in the Parish of St. Nicholas Withycombe, Somerset, 1670-1710
  www.genuki.org.uk/big/eng/SOM/Withycombe/MarWit1670.html
  Continued to 1841 on 4 further pages

- Withycombe, Somerset: Banns 1754-1813
  www.genuki.org.uk/big/eng/SOM/Withycombe/17541813.banns.txt
  Continued 1824-1903 at /18241903_banns.txt

- Burials in the Parish of St. Nicholas, Withycombe, Somerset, 1669-1699
  www.genuki.org.uk/big/eng/SOM/Withycombe/BurWit1669.html
  Continued to 1812 on 2 further pages

Wiveliscombe
- Menu for Extracts from Wiveliscombe Parish Register and Independent Church Register: Index
  www.btinternet.com/~PBenyon/H_m_w/Wiv/Index.html

- Extracts from Wiveliscombe Parish Baptisms
  freepages.genealogy.rootsweb.com/~pbtyc/H_m_w/Wiv/Wiv_Bap_Bab_Bur.html
  Alphabetical. Continued on 9 further pages

- Extracts from Wiveliscombe Parish Register: Banns
  freepages.genealogy.rootsweb.com/~pbtyc/H_m_w/Wiv/Ban/Wiv_Ban_All_Col.htm
  Alphabetical. Continued on 4 further pages

- Extracts from Wiveliscombe, Somerset, Parish Register: Marriages
  freepages.genealogy.rootsweb.com/~pbtyc/H_m_w/Wiv/Mar/A-Chi.html
  Alphabetical. Continued on 6 further pages

- Extracts from Wiveliscombe, Somerset, Parish Register: Burials
  freepages.genealogy.rootsweb.com/~pbtyc/H_m_w/Wiv/Bur/Ans_ChoA.html
  Alphabetical. Continued on 6 further pages

- Names Extracted from the Burial Register for the Parish of Wiveliscombe, Somerset, 1826-1838
  www.genuki.org.uk/big/eng/SOM/Wiveliscombe/Burials1826-1838.txt

Worle
- Worle Baptism Records, 1813-1837
  www.freeuk.net/wsmfhs/worlebaptism.htm
  Index to a published transcript

- Worle Burial Records, 1813-1837
  home.freeuk.net/wsmfhs/worleburial.htm
  Index to a published transcript

Yarlington
- Yarlington, Somerset Marriages 1601 to 1754
  www.westcountrygenealogy.com/somerset/yarlington_marriages.htm

Surrey

Civil Registration
- Registration Districts in Surrey
  www.fhsc.org.uk/genuki/reg/sry.htm
  Between 1837 and 1930

- [St. Catherine's House Marriage Index, Jan-March, 1849. District 4: Surrey *etc.*]
  www.cs.ncl.ac.uk/genuki/StCathsTranscriptions/CATH4904.TXT

Parish & Non-Parochial Registers: Introductory Pages & Lists
- Parish Registers
  shs.surreycc.gov.uk
  Click on 'Topics' and title. General discussion for Surrey

- Guide to Parish Registers held at Surrey History Centre
  shs.surreycc.govuk/fhparint.html
  List of original registers, transcripts, microfilm, *etc.*

- Index to Parish Register Holdings in the Archive & Local Studies Searchroom
  www.sutton.gov.uk/lfl/heritage/als/parishes.html
  List of registers on fiche at Sutton Library, mainly for Surrey, but also for Thames riverside parishes in Essex, Kent and Middlesex

- Surrey
  www.sog.org.uk/prc/surrey.html
  Parish registers, printed, typescript, *etc.,* in the library of the Society of Genealogists

- Quaker Family History Society: Surrey
  www.rootsweb.com/~engqfhs/Research/counties/surrey.htm
  Notes on Quaker records

Indexes
- IGI Batch Numbers: Surrey Batch Numbers
  freepages.genealogy.rootsweb.com/~tyeroots/surrey.html

- IGI Batch Numbers for Surrey, England
  freepages.genealogy.rootsweb.com/~hughwallis/IGIBatchNumbers/CountySurrey.htm

Publications
- East Surrey Family History Society Bookstall
  www.eastsurreyfhs.org.uk/publics.htm
  Includes parish registers, etc.

Lookups
- Parish Register Lookups
  www.artscape.demon.co.uk/SRYexchange/parreg.html

Albury
- Parish of St. Peter and St. Paul, Albury, and St. Michael
  www.alburychurches.webapt.co.uk/
  Register of burials from 1913; also memorials

Croydon
- Croydon Council Home Page: Parish Registers
  www.croydon.gov.uk/LEDept/localstudies/REGISTERS.HTM
  List of registers held at Croydon Local Studies Library for Croydon, Addington, Coulsdon and Sanderstead

Sussex

Civil Registration
- Registration Districts in Sussex
  www.fhsc.org.uk/genuki/reg/ssx.htm
  Between 1837 and 1930

- Registration of Births Marriages and Deaths
  www.eastsussex.gov.uk/reg/main.htm
  With addresses of offices in East Sussex

Parish & Non-Parochial Registers: Introductory Pages & Lists
- West Sussex Record Office: Family History: Parish Registers
  www.westsussex.gov.uk/RO/FamHis/FH%20parish%20rec.htm
  Includes list

- West Sussex Record Office: Bishops' Transcripts
  www.westsussex.gov.uk/RO/FamHis/FHBishopts.htm

- West Sussex Record Office: Family History: Nonconformist Registers
  www.westsussex.gov.uk/RO/FamHis/FHnon%20con.htm
  General discussion

- Sussex
  www.sog.org.uk/prc/ssx.html
  Parish registers, printed, typescript, *etc.*, in the library of the Society of Genealogists

- Hastings and Rother Family History Society: Parish Register Dates
  www.hrfhs.org.uk/main.htm
  Click on 'parish registers'. In the Hastings area

- Quaker Family History Society: Sussex
  www.rootsweb.com/~engqfhs/Research/counties/sussex.htm
  Notes on Quaker records

Indexes
- Sussex Baptismal Index
  www.sfhg.org.uk/baptisms.html
  Brief note on a Sussex Family History Group index still in its early stages of compilation

- Sussex Marriages
  www.srichards.freeserve.co.uk/gen-parish%20registers-sussex-marriages.txt
  Index for selected names and parishes

- The Sussex Marriage Index 1538-1837
  www.sfhg.org.uk/marriageindex.html
  Description of a major offline index held by Sussex Family History Group

- IGI Batch Numbers: Sussex Batch Numbers
  freepages.genealogy.rootsweb.com/~tyeroots/sussex.html

- IGI Batch Numbers for Sussex, England
  freepages.genealogy.rootsweb.com/~hughwallis/IGIBatchNumbers/CountySussex.htm

Publications
- The Institute of Historical and Genealogical Studies: The Sussex Collection
  www.ihgs.ac.uk/library/sussex_collection.php
  List of register indexes *etc.*, on fiche

- Sussex Family History Group Publications
  www.sfhg.org.uk/pubs_sfhg.html
  Includes some parish registers and microfiche, *etc.*

- PBN Publications
  www.pbnpublications.com/
  Many Sussex published parish registers and monumental inscriptions for sale

- West Sussex Record Office: Parish Registers Transcripts
  www.westsussex.gov.uk/RO/FamHis/parishgreg_trans.htm
  Transcripts available on fiche

- West Sussex Record Office: Parish Registers on Fiche
  www.westsussex.gov.uk/RO/FamHis/parish_fiche.htm
  Original registers available on fiche

Wiltshire

Civil registration
See also Dorset

- Registration Districts in Wiltshire
  www.fhsc.org.uk/genuki/reg/wil.htm
  Between 1837 and 1930

Parish & Non-Parochial Registers: Introductory Pages & Lists
- Wiltshire
  www.sog.org.uk/prc/wiltshire.html
  Parish registers, printed, typescript, *etc.,* in the library of the Society of Genealogists

- Quaker Family History Society: Wiltshire
  www.rootsweb.com/~engqfhs/Research/counties/wilts.htm
  Notes on Quaker records

- Wiltshire Monthly Meeting (Quaker) 1657-1837
  www.wis.mcmail.com/quaker.htm
  Marriage partners; surnames only

Indexes
- IGI Batch Numbers: Wiltshire Batch Numbers
  freepages.genealogy.rootsweb.com/~tyeroots/wiltshire.html

- IGI Batch Numbers for Wiltshire, England
  freepages.genealogy.rootsweb.com/~hughwallis/IGIBatchNumbers/CountyWiltshire.htm

- Wiltshire's Nimrod Indexes
  www.redbreast.co.uk/nimrod/
  Commercial indexes of baptisms and burials, and marriages, *etc.*

Publications
- Wiltshire Family History Society: Parish Registers
  www.genuki.org.uk/big/eng/WIL/WSFHS/Transcripts.htm
  List of published registers

Transcript Collections on the Web
- Wiltshire Parish Marriage Index
  www.wis.mcmail.com/ring.htm
  Collection of web-pages, listed separately below. Also includes listing of registers in *Phillimore's Parish Register* series for Wiltshire

Alton Barnes
- Alton Barnes 1597-1837
  www.wis.mcmail.com/abarnes.htm
  Surnames only, from the parish register

Ashley
- Ashley 1607-1837 A-Z
  www.wis.mcmail.com/ashley.htm
  Surnames only, from the parish register

Bishopstone
- Bishopstone (North) 1573-1837 A-Z
  www.wis.mcmail.com/bishopsn.htm
  Surnames only, from the parish register

Blunsdon St. Andrew
- Blunsdon St Andrew 1655-1837
  www.wis.mcmail.com/blstandw.htm
  Surnames only, from the parish register

Brinkworth
- Brinkworth Baptisms 1659-1856
  www.genuki.org.uk/big/eng/WIL/Brinkworth/BRINKC-A.htm
  Continued on 6 further pages
- Brinkworth Marriage Banns Name Index: Banns 1754-1809
  www.genuki.org.uk/big/eng/WIL/Brinkworth/BRINKBN-A.htm
  Continued at **/BRINKBN-M.htm**
- Brinkworth Marriages and Banns Name Index: Marriages 1653-1839
  www.genuki.org.uk/big/eng/WIL/Brinkworth/BRINKM-A.htm
  Continued on 4 further pages
- Brinkworth Burials Name Index 1653-1883
  www.genuki.org.uk/big/eng/WIL/Brinkworth/BRINKB-A.htm
  Continued on 3 further pages

Burbage
- Burbage Family History
  www.keble.clara.net/burbage.htm
  Includes baptisms 1662-1864, marriages 1800-1821, burials 1661-1834, *etc.*

Chilmark
- Chilmark 1611-1837 A-Z
  www.wis.mcmail.com/chilmark.htm
  Surnames only, from the parish register

Chirton
- Chirton 1588-1837 A-Z
  www.wis.mcmail.com/chirton.htm
  Surnames only, from the parish register

Corsham
- Corsham 1563-1837 A-Z
  www.wis.mcmail.com/corsham.htm
  Surnames only, from the parish register

Cricklade
- Friends of St. Mary's Church, Cricklade, Wiltshire, UK: Registers
  www.tetlow.screaming.net/registers.htm
  Marriages, 1686-1909

Devizes
- Index of Births at the Devizes Workhouse: Parish of Devizes, County of Wiltshire, England 1848-1902
  thor.prohosting.com/~hughw/Devizesb.txt
- Index of Deaths at the Devizes Workhouse: Parish of Devizes, County of Wiltshire, England 1866-1902
  thor.prohosting.com/~hughw/Devizesd.txt

Etchilhampton
- Etchilhampton 1630-1837 A-Z
  www.wis.mcmail.com/etch.htm
  Surnames only, from the parish register

Holyrood
- Holyrood (Swindon) 1590-1622 A-Z
  www.wis.mcmail.com/holyrood.htm
  Surnames only, from the parish register

Long Newnton
- Long Newnton 1609-1837 A-Z
  www.wis.mcmail.com/newnton.htm
  Surnames only, from the parish register

Patney
- Patney 1594-1837 A-Z
  www.wis.mcmail.com/patney.htm
  Surnames only, from the parish register

Plaitford
- Plaitford 1622-1836 A-Z
  www.wis.mcmail.com/Plaitford.htm
  Surnames only, from the parish register

Pool Keynes
- Pool Keynes 1605-1837 A-Z
  www.wis.mcmail.com/PlKeynes.htm
  Surnames only, from the parish register

Salisbury
- Salisbury Cathedral 1570-1837 A-Z
  www.wis.mcmail.com/salcath.htm
  Surnames only, from the parish register

- Brown St. Particular Baptist Chapel, Salisbury
  homepages.rootsweb.com/~mwi/baptisms.txt
  Births register, 18-19th c.

Stanton Fitzwarren
- Stanton Fitzwarren 1543-1837 A-Z
  www.wis.mcmail.com/fitzwarn.htm
  Surnames only, from the parish register

Stert
- Stert 1579-1837 A-Z
  www.wis.mcmail.com/stert.htm
  Surnames only, from the parish register

Stratton St. Margaret
- Stratton St Margaret 1608-1837 A-Z
  www.wis.mcmail.com/ssmargt.htm
  Surnames only, from the parish register

Swindon
- Swindon Christ Church 1624-1837
  www.wis.mcmail.com/swindncc.htm
  Surnames only, from the parish register

Worcestershire

Civil Registration
- Registration Districts in Worcestershire
  www.fhsc.org.uk/genuki/reg/wor.htm
  Between 1837 and 1930

Parish & Non-Parochial Registers: Introductory Pages & Lists
- Parish Registers on Microfilm
  www.worcestershire.gov.uk/home/cs-records-a-h.pdf
  Continued at /cs-records-i-y.pdf See also /cs-records-notes2.pdf
  At Worcestershire Record Office
- The Parishes of Worcestershire
  www.geocities.com/Heartland/Plains/8555/worpar.html
  Locations and commencement dates of parish registers
- Parish Registers held at Birmingham Central Library
  www.spencer.onlinehome.de/registers.html
  Includes registers, transcripts, fiche, *etc.*, for Staffordshire, Warwickshire and Worcestershire. Does not list the substantial collection of published registers from other counties.
- Worcestershire
  www.sog.org.uk/pro/worcestershire.htm
  Parish registers, printed, typescript *etc.*, in the library of the Society of Genealogists
- Quaker Family History Society: Worcestershire
  www.rootsweb.com/~engqfhs/Research/counties/worcs.htm
  Notes on Quaker records
- B.M.S.G.H. Search Services
  www.bmsgh.org/search/seal.html
  Details of various marriage and burial indexes for Staffordshire, Warwickshire and Worcestershire
- Privately Owned Indexes Relating to Staffordshire, Warwickshire or Worcestershire
  www.bmsgh.org.uk/search/sea4.html
  Lists various indexes to parish registers

- IGI Batch Numbers: Worcestershire Batch Numbers
  freepages.genealogy.rootsweb.com/~tyeroots/worcest.html
- IGI Batch Numbers for Worcester, England
  freepages.genealogy.rootsweb.com/~hughwallis/IGIBatchNumbers/CountyWorcester.htm
- Free Reg: Worcestershire
  freereg.rootsweb.com/parishes/wor/index.htm
  Details of the project to index births, marriages and deaths

Publications
- B.M.S.G.H. Bookshop: Worcestershire: Parishes, Census Districts & other places
  www.bmsgh.org/bookshop/worc/wo.a.html
  List of parish registers, monumental inscriptions, *etc.*, published as books and fiche

Badsey
- Badsey St. James Parish
  www.badsey.net/history/index.htm
  Includes parish registers, 1530-1909
  See also Wickhamford

Blackheath
- St. Paul's, Blackheath, Halesowen: Marriages 1919-1927
  uk-transcriptions.accessgenealogy.com/St.Paul's,Blackheath%20Marriages.htm

Blockley
- Blockley Baptisms; Blockley Marriages; Blockley Burials
  members.shaw.ca/panthers1/BlockleyRecords.html
  Baptisms 1538-1812; marriages 1539-1978; burials 1538-1812

Cradley
- Cradley Parish Registers
  web.bham.ac.uk/P.A.Beasley/CradleyParReg.htm
  Baptisms 1785-1808; Burials 1785-1820 & 1843-4. More forthcoming
- Cradley Links: Parish Register Search
  www.cradleylinks.com/parish_registers.html
  Database

Dudley
- St. Edmond's, Dudley: Marriages 1870-1879
  uk-transcriptions.accessgenealogy.com/St.Edmond's.Dudley.htm

- St. Thomas, Dudley: Baptisms, Marriages & Burials
  uk-transcriptions.accessgenealogy.com/St.Thomas.Dudley.htm
  19th c.

Halesowen
- St. John's Church of England, Halesowen, Worcestershire Parish Registers
  www.platt-grigg.accessgenealogy.com/custom3.html
  1717-28

- St. John's, Halesowen: Baptisms, Marriages & Burials
  uk-transcriptions.accessgenealogy.com/St.John's.Halesowen.htm
  Mainly 18-19th c.

- St. John's, Halesowen 1720-1721: Parish Registers of the Church of St. John the Baptist, Halesowen: Baptisms / Marriages / Burials 1717-1736
  uk-transcriptions.accessgenealogy.com/St.John's%201717-1736.txt
  Incomplete
  See also Blackheath

Netherton
- St. Andrew's, Netherton: Baptisms, Marriages & Burials
  uk-transcriptions.accessgenealogy.com/St.Andrew's.Netherton.htm
  1846-1983

Wickhamford
- Wickhamford Baptismal Registers: connections with Badsey
  www.badsey.net/history/wford.htm
  Covers 1546-1856

Wales

Civil Registration
- Wales: Civil Registration
  www.genuki.org.uk/big/wal/CivilRegistration.html
  Links

- [St.Catherine's House Marriage Index, Jan-March, 1849. District 27. Wales
  www.cs.ncl.ac.uk/genuki/StCathsTranscriptions/CATH4927.TXT

- [St.Catherine's House Marriage Index, Jan-March, 1849. District 26. Wales/Herefordshire, *etc.*]
  www.cs.ncl.ac.uk/genuki/StCathsTranscriptions/CATH4926.TXT

Parish & Non-Parochial Register: Introductory Pages & Lists
- Church in Wales Records
  www.llgc.org.uk/ht/ht__s008.htm
  Notes on parish registers, bishops' transcripts, marriage bonds, *etc.,* at the National Library of Wales

- Wales
  www.sog.org.uk/prc/wal.html
  Parish registers, printed, typescript, *etc.,* in the library of the Society of Genealogists.

- Quaker Family History Society: Wales (including Monmouthshire)
  www.rootsweb.com/~engqfhs/Research/counties/wales.htm
  Notes on Quaker records

Indexes
- IGI Batch Numbers: Wales Batch Numbers
  freepages.genealogy.rootsweb.com/~tyeroots/index7.html

Marriage Licences
- Marriage Bonds and Allegations
  www.llgc.org.uk/lc/lc0052.htm
  Detailed descriptions, with notes on an index

Anglesey

Civil Registration
- Registration District in Anglesey
  www.fhsc.org.uk/genuki/reg/agy.htm
  Between 1837 and 1930

Parish & Non-Parochial Registers: Introductory Pages & Lists
- Anglesey County Record Office: A list of the Parish Registers in the Anglesey County Record Office
  www.ynosmon.gov.uk/english/library/archives/register.htm

- Anglesey Parish Registers
  www.genuki.org.uk/big/wal/AGY/AGY__PR.html
  Held by Anglesey Record Office

- Calvinistic Methodist Births/Baptisms, Anglesey (pre1837)
  www.genuki.org.uk/big/wal/AGY/MethBaps/

- Wesleyan Methodist Births/Baptisms, Holyhead Circuit, 1842-1890
  www.genuki.org.uk/big/wal/AGY/MethBaps/WesBaps.html

- Wesleyan Methodist Baptisms/Births in the Beaumaris Circuit
  www.genuki.org.uk/big/wal/AGY/MethBaps/WesBeau.html
  Early 19th c.

Indexes
- IGI Batch Numbers for Anglesey, Wales
  freepages.genealogy.rootsweb.com/~hughwallis/IGIBatchNumbers/CountyAnglesey.htm

Publications
- Gwynedd Family History Society: Society Publication and Research Information
  www.gwynedd.fsbusiness.co.uk
  Click on 'Publications'. Includes indexes to baptisms and marriages, monumental inscriptions, *etc.*, for Anglesey, Caernarvonshire and Merionethshire

Breconshire

Civil Registration
- Registrars of Births, Marriages and Deaths
  archives.powys.gov.uk/lsn/12.html
  In Powys

- Registration Districts in Breconshire
  www.fhsc.org.uk/genuki/reg/bre.htm
  Between 1837 and 1930

Parish & Non-Parochial Registers: Introductory Pages & Lists
- Breconshire Parish Registers
  archives.powys.gov.uk/lsn/01.html
  List of microfilmed copies at the Powys County Archives Office

- Nonconformist Records
  archives.powys.gov.uk/hold/non.html
  At Powys Record Office; including registers

Indexes
- Powys F.H.S. Resources and Indexes
  www.rootsweb.com/~wlspfhs/powysnbi.htm
  Includes details of Powys Burials Index, covering parts of Breconshire, Montgomeryshire and Radnorshire

- IGI Batch Numbers for Brecon, Wales
  freepages.genealogy.rootsweb.com/~hughwallis/IGIBatchNumbers/CountyBrecon.htm

St. Illtyd
- Burials 1813 to 1930 scanned in January 2002 by Friends of St. Illtyd
  www.onetell.net.uk/~hywelc/burials/burialsm2.htm

Caernarvonshire

Civil Registration
- Registration Districts in Caernarvonshire
  www.fhsc.org.uk/genuki/reg/cae.htm
  Between 1837 and 1930

Parish & Non-Parochial Registers: Introductory Pages & Lists
- Caernarfonshire Parish Registers
  www.genuki.org.uk/big/wal/CAE/CAE__PR.html
  List of registers (including microfilm) at Caernarfon Area Record Offices

Indexes
- IGI Batch Numbers for Caernarvon, Wales
  freepages.genealogy.rootsweb.com/~hughwallis/IGIBatchNumbers/CountyCaernarvon.htm

Publications
See Anglesey

Cardiganshire

Civil Registration
- Registration Districts in Cardiganshire
  www.fhsc.org.uk/genuki/reg/cgn.htm
  Between 1837 and 1930

Parish & Non-Parochial Registers: Introductory Pages & Lists
- Register Repositories: Registers of Cardiganshire
  www.dyfedfhs.org.uk/copi.htm
  Click on county. List of registers with locations

Indexes
- Three Counties Marriages 1813-1837 by Grooms Index
  www.rootsweb.com/~wlscfhs/threecountiesmarriages.htm
  For Cardiganshire, Carmarthenshire and Pembrokeshire

- Cardiganshire, Wales, Marriage Index (1813-1837)
  www.dyfedfhs.org.uk/copi.htm
  On-line index to 10,380 grooms

- Cardiganshire Marriages 1813-1837
  www.rootsweb.com/~wlscfhs/cdgmarr.pdf

- IGI Batch Numbers for Cardigan, Wales
  freepages.genealogy.rootsweb.com/~hughwallis/IGIBatchNumbers/CountyCardigan.htm

Publications
- Dyfed FHS Publications
  www.dyfedfhs.org.uk/copi.htm
  Click on 'publications'. Includes many registers and monumental inscriptions, *etc.,* on fiche

- Indexes and Transcripts for Sale on Fiche: Baptisms, Marriages and Burials
  www.westwales.co.uk/dfhs/forsale1.htm
  From Dyfed Family History Society, covering Cardiganshire, Carmarthenshire and Pembrokeshire

- Indexes for Sale on Fiche: the Merlin Indexes
  www.westwales.co.uk/dfhs/forsale4.htm
  Index to baptisms, marriages and burials, *etc.,* for Carmarthenshire, from Dyfed Family History Society

Aberystwyth
See Llangynfelyn

Elerch
- Eglwys St. Peter's Church, Elerch, Ceredigion/Cardiganshire ...: Baptism Records
  freepages.genealogy.rootsweb.com/~ceredigwynd/stpeters-baptism.html
  Covers 1865-1910

- Eglwys St. Peter's Church, Elerch, Ceredigion/Cardiganshire
  freepages.genealogy.rootsweb.com/~ceredigwynd/stpeters-wedding.html
  Marriages, 1868-99

- Eglwys St. Peter's Church, Elerch, Ceredigion/Cardiganshire: Burials Records
  freepages.genealogy.rootsweb.com/~ceredigwynd/stpeters-burial.htm
  Covers 1868-91

Llangynfelyn
- Aberystwyth Wesleyan Circuit: Baptisms 1815-1837
  www.llangynfelyn.co.uk/dogfennau/ npr_wesleyan_aber_circuit_bedydd.html
  Entries for Llangynfellyn

- Baptisms by Azariah Shadrach (Independent) 1811-1821
  www.llangynfelyn.dabsol.co.uk/dogfennau/npr_shadrach_bedydd.html
  At Llangynfelyn

Taliesin
- Rehoboth Chapel, Taliesin Baptisms 1812-1850
  www.llangynfelyn.dabsol.co.uk/cma_rehob.bedydd.html

Carmarthenshire

Civil Registration
- Registration Districts in Carmarthenshire
  www.fhsc.org.uk/genuki/reg/cmn.htm
  Between 1837 & 1930

Parish & Non-Parochial Registers: Introductory Pages & Lists
- Register Repositories: Registers of Carmarthenshire
  www.dyfedfhs.org.uk/copi.htm
  Click on county. List of registers with locations

Indexes
See also Carmarthenshire
- IGI Batch Numbers for Carmarthen, Wales
  freepages.genealogy.rootsweb.com/~hughwallis/IGIBatchNumbers/ CountyCarmarthen.htm

Publications
See Cardiganshire

Carmarthen
- Carmarthen St. Peter's Baptisms 1722-1801
  www.rootsweb.com/~wlscfhs/cmnbaps1722-1801.PDF

- Carmarthen St. Peter's Marriages 1813-1837
  www.rootsweb.com/~wlscfhs/cmnmarriages1813-1837.PDF

- Carmarthen St. Peter's Burials 1671-1801
  www.rootsweb.com/~wlscfhs/cmnburials1671-1801.PDF

Kidwelly
- Kidwelly Parish Burials 1813-1837
  www.rootsweb.com/~wlscfhs/kidburials.PDF

Llanegwad
- Llanegwad: The Parish Records
  www.llanegwad-carmarthen.co.uk/prfacts.htm
  Off-line index

Llanelli
- Llanelli St. Elli Parish Church Baptisms 1813-1832
  www.rootsweb.com/~wlscfhs/llanbaps13-37.PDF

- Llanelli St. Elli Parish Church Marriages 1813-1837
  www.rootsweb.com/~wlscfhs/llanmars.PDF

- Llanelli Marriages 1833-1837, St. Elli Parish Church, Llanelli Marriages 1864-1867 taken from *Llanelli Guardian* births, deaths and marriages
  ftp.rootsweb.com/pub/wggenweb/wales/vital/llanelli.txt

- Llanelli St. Elli Parish Church Burials 1813-1837
  www.rootsweb.com/~wlscfhs/llanburs.PDF

Pembrey
- Pembrey Parish Baptisms 1813-1831
  www.rootsweb.com/~wlscfhs/ppbaptisms.PDF

- Pembrey Parish Marriages 1813-1837
  www.rootsweb.com/~wlscfhs/ppmarriages.PDF

- Pembrey Parish Burials 1800-1837
  www.rootsweb.com/~wlscfhs/ppburials.PDF

Flint and Denbighshire

Civil Registration
- Registration Districts covering Denbighshire, as established on 1 July 1837
  www.genuki.org.uk/big/wal/DEN/RegDistricts/index.html

- Registration Districts in Flintshire
  www.fhsc.org.uk/genuki/reg/ftn.htm
  Between 1837 & 1930

Parish & Non-Parochial Registers: Introductory Pages & Lists
- Parish Registers: Background Information
  www.clwydfhs.org.uk/registers/background.html
  For Flintshire and Denbighshire

Indexes
- IGI Batch Numbers for Denbigh, Wales
  freepages.genealogy.rootsweb.com/~hughwallis/IGIBatchNumbers/CountyDenbigh.htm

- IGI Batch Numbers for Flint, Wales
  freepages.genealogy.rootsweb.com/~hughwallis/IGIBatchNumbers/CountyFlint.htm

Publications
- Clwyd Family History Society: Transcriptions of Parish Registers
  www.clwydfhs.org.uk/registers/index.html
  List of transcripts for sale as booklets or fiche for Flintshire and Denbighshire

Glamorganshire

Civil Registration
- Registration Districts in Glamorganshire
  www.fhsc.org.uk/genuki/reg/gla.htm
  Between 1837 & 1930

Parish & Non-Parochial registers: Introductory Pages & Lists
- An Index to the Registers of the Methodist Churches of Glamorgan
  www.angelfire.com/ga/BobSanders/METHREC1.html
  List with locations

- An index to the Records of the Non-Conformist (excl.Methodist) Churches of Glamorgan
  www.angelfire.com/ga/BobSanders/NONCON1.html
  Continued at **/NONCON2.html** and **/NONCON3.html** List of registers with locations

- Parish Records and Non-Parochial Records held at Cardiff Central Library
  home.clara.net/tirbach/HelpPaseCardiffDirs.html#Parish Records

Indexes
- IGI Batch Numbers for Glamorgan, Wales
  freepages.genealogy.rootsweb.com/~hughwallis/IGIBatchNumbers/CountyGlamorgan.htm

Publications
- Glamorgan Family History Society Booklet Publications: Parish Registers
  www.rootsweb.com/~wlsglfhs/books1.htm

- Glamorgan Family History Society Microfiche Publications
  www.rootsweb.com/~wlsglfhs/fiche1.htm
  Includes church and chapel registers

Cardiff
- Cardiff Non-Conformist Registers
  www.genuki.org.uk/big/wal/GLA/Cardiff/Nonconformist.html
  List with locations

- Cardiff Records volume III, chapter X: Parochial Records
  www.btinternet.com/~pat.sewell/cr/cr-parochial-records.html
  Includes index to registers of St. John's, Cardiff 1669-1772, and Roath, 1731-1845

Roath
See Cardiff

Swansea
- Swansea Non-Conformist Registers
  www.genuki.org.uk/big/wal/GLA/Swansea/nonconformist.html
  List with locations

Merionethshire

Civil Registration
- Registration Districts in Merionethshire
  www.fhsc.org.uk/genuki/reg/mer.htm
  Between 1837 & 1930

Parish & Non-Parochial Registers: Introductory Pages & Lists
- Merionethshire Parish Registers
  www.genuki.org.uk/big/wal/MER/MER__PR.html
  List with locations

Indexes
- IGI Batch Numbers for Merioneth, Wales
  freepages.genealogy.rootsweb.com/~hughwallis/IGIBatchNumbers/CountyMerioneth.htm

Publications
See Anglesey

Monmouthshire

Civil Registration
- Registration Districts in Monmouthshire
  www.fhsc.org.uk/genuki/reg/mon.htm
  Between 1837 & 1930

Parish & Non-Parochial Registers: Introductory Pages & Lists
- List of Monmouthshire Transcriptions
  www.genuki.org.uk/big/wal/MON/PR__List.html
  Parish register transcripts held by the Society of Genealogists

Indexes
- Free Reg: Monmouthshire
  freereg.rootsweb.com/parishes/mon/index.htm
  Details of the registers currently included in the project to index births, deaths and marriages

- Enquiry Services and other facilities
  www.rootsweb.com/~wlsgfhs/Services.htm
  Details of Gwent Family History Society's marriage and burial indexes

- Monmouthshire Marriages 1725-1812: Grooms Surname Index
  freepages.genealogy.rootsweb.com/~monfamilies/Monmarrindex.html

- IGI Batch Numbers for Monmouth, England
  freepages.genealogy.rootsweb.com/~hughwallis/IGIBatchNumbers/CountyMonmouth.htm

Publications
- Church and Chapel Registers
  www.rootsweb.com/~wlsgfhs/Sales/Registers.htm
  Available on fiche or CD from Gwent Family History Society

Tintern Parva
- The Parish Church of St. Michael and All Angels, Tintern Parva, with the church of Saint Mary, Chapel Hill, Diocese of Monmouth
  www.tintern.co.uk/membook.htm
  Burials from 1813 for Tintern, and from 1880 for Chapel Hill

Montgomeryshire

See also Breconshire

Civil Registration
- Registration Districts in Montgomeryshire
  www.fhsc.org.uk/genuki/reg/mgy.htm
  Between 1837 & 1930

Parish & Non-Parochial Registers: Introductory Pages & Lists
- Montgomeryshire Parish Registers
  archives.powys.gov.uk/lsn/02.html
  List of microfilms held at Powys Record Office

Indexes
- IGI Batch Numbers for Montgomery, Wales
  freepages.genealogy.rootsweb.com/~hughwallis/IGIBatchNumbers/CountyMontgomery.htm

Publications
- Montgomeryshire Family History Society Publications
  home.freeuk.net/montgensoc/pages/pubns.htm
  Includes registers, inscriptions, *etc.*

Pembrokeshire

Civil Registration
- Registration Districts in Pembrokeshire
  www.fhsc.org.uk/genuki/reg/pem.htm
  Between 1837 & 1930

Parish & Non-Parochial Registers: Introductory Pages & Lists
- Register Repositories: Registers of Pembrokeshire
  www.dyfedfhs.org.uk/copi.htm
  Click on county. List of registers with locations

Indexes
See also Carmarthenshire
- Pembrokeshire Marriages 1813-1837
  www.rootsweb.com/~wlscfhs/pembsmarrs.pdf
- IGI Batch Numbers for Pembroke, Wales
  freepages.genealogy.rootsweb.com/~hughwallis/IGIBatchNumbers/CountyPembroke.htm

Publications
See Cardiganshire

Angle
- Parish of Angle: Marriages 1813-1837
  members.lycos.co.uk/Graham__Davies/Cas100/AngleMarr.html

Bosherston
- Bosherston Church: Baptism Register
  www.stackpole.freeserve.co.uk/bobap.htm
  Index 18-20th c.

- Bosherston Church: Marriage Register
  www.stackpole.freeserve.co.uk/bowed.htm
  Index, 18-20th c.

- Bosherston Church: Burial Register
  www.stackpole.freeserve.co.uk/bobur.htm
  Index, 18-20th c.

Castlemartin
- Parish of Castlemartin: Marriages
  members.lycos.co.uk/Graham__Davies/Cas100/CastlemartinMarr.html
  1813-37

St. Petrox
- St. Petrox Church: Baptism Register
  www.stackpole.freeserve.co.uk/pebap.htm
  Index 17-20th c.

- St. Petrox Church: Marriage Register
  www.stackpole.freeserve.co.uk/pewed.htm
  Index, 17-20th c.

- St. Petrox Church: Burial Register
  www.stackpole.freeserve.co.uk/pebur.htm
  Index, 17-20th c.

St. Twynnells
- St. Twynnells Church: Baptism Register
  www.stackpole.freeserve.co.uk/twbap.htm
  Index, 18-20th c.

- St. Twynnells Church: Marriage Register
  www.stackpole.freeserve.co.uk/twwed.htm
  Index, 18-20th c.

- St. Twynnells Church: Burial Register
  www.stackpole.freeserve.co.uk/twbur.htm
  Index 18-20th c.

Stackpole
- Stackpole Elidor Church: Baptism Register
  www.stackpole.freeserve.co.uk/stbap.htm
  Index 18-20th c.

- Stackpole Elidor Church: Marriage Register
  www.stackpole.freeserve.co.uk/stwed.htm
  Index, 18-20th c.

- Stackpole Elidor Church: Burial Register
  www.stackpole.freeserve.co.uk/stbur.htm
  Index, 18-20th c.

Radnorshire

See also Breconshire

Civil Registration
- Registration Districts in Radnorshire
  www.fhsc.org.uk/genuki/reg/rad.htm
  Between 1837 & 1930

Parish & Non-Parochial Registers: Introductory Pages & Lists
- Radnorshire Parish Registers
  archives.powys.gov.uk/lsn/03.html
  List of microfilmed registers held at Powys Record Office

Indexes
- IGI Batch Numbers for Radnor, Wales
  freepages.genealogy.rootsweb.com/~hughwallis/IGIBatchNumbers/CountyRadnor.htm